THE **MINI** ROUGH GUIDE TO
DUBLIN

YOUR TAILOR-MADE TRIP
STARTS HERE

Tailor-made trips and unique adventures crafted by local experts

Rough Guides has been inspiring travellers for more than 35 years. Leave it to our local experts to create your perfect itinerary and book it at local rates.

Don't follow the crowd – find your own path.

HOW ROUGHGUIDES.COM/TRIPS WORKS

STEP 1 Pick your dream destination, tell us what you want and submit an enquiry.

STEP 2 Fill in a short form to tell your local expert about your dream trip and preferences.

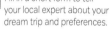

STEP 3 Our local expert will craft your tailor-made itinerary. You'll be able to tweak and refine it until you're completely satisfied.

STEP 4 Book online with ease, pack your bags and enjoy the trip! Our local expert will be on hand 24/7 while you're on the road.

PLAN AND BOOK YOUR TRIP AT
ROUGHGUIDES.COM/TRIPS

HOW TO DOWNLOAD YOUR FREE EBOOK

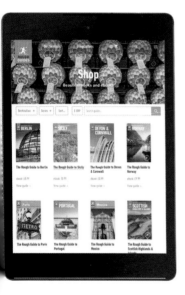

1. Visit **www.roughguides.com/free-ebook** or scan the **QR code** below

2. Enter the code **dublin755**

3. Follow the simple step-by-step instructions

For troubleshooting contact: mail@roughguides.com

10 THINGS NOT TO MISS

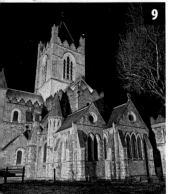

A PERFECT DAY

8:30am

Breakfast. Sweet or savoury, *Lemon Crepe & Coffee Co* (66 South William Street) has an array of breakfast crepes, pancakes, Belgian waffles and exceptional coffee that will set you up perfectly for a day of sightseeing.

9:30am

City treasures. Walk north on William Street South and on to St Andrews Street – Dublin's famous fishwife 'Molly Malone' is on the corner. Continue along Church Street, then turn on to College Green to get to Trinity College. By arriving early you should avoid the crowds that flock to see the magnificent library and its illuminated manuscript, the Book of Kells.

11:30am

Oriental Café. Walk up Grafton Street and relax over a coffee at Bewley's, surrounded by the stained-glass windows of this art-deco icon.

12 noon

Exploration. Browse the Grafton Street shops as you proceed south towards St Stephen's Green. After a stroll on the green, head along the north side, perhaps investigating curios at The Little Museum of Dublin, then turn left onto Kildare Street for Leinster House, the Museum of Ireland – Archaeology, and the National Library of Ireland. Turn left on to Molesworth Street and left on to Dawson Street for lunch at Café en Seine (39–40 Dawson Street).

IN DUBLIN

2:30pm

To the river. Turn left at the bottom of Dawson Street and veer around the front of Trinity College on to Westmoreland Street. At the end turn left to take a stroll along the River Liffey, pausing to glance at the charming Ha'Penny Bridge. Continue and turn left up Winetavern Street just beyond the Civic Offices.

3:30pm

Major landmarks. At the top of the street is Christ Church Cathedral, it is well worth a visit. Then make your way via Christchurch Place and Lord Edward Street for a peek at Dublin Castle.

5:00pm

Pit-stop. Cross the road from the castle and go back up the hill. Turn into Cow's Lane with its craft shops and the Queen of Tarts, the perfect pit stop for tea and home-baked treats.

7:30pm

Evening meal. After freshening up at your hotel, return to Dame Street and Forno 500° (No. 74 – next door to the Olympia Theatre) for delicious Neapolitan sourdough pizza in a relaxed Dublin setting.

9:30pm

On the town. Turn left out of the restaurant and take the second left on to Eustace Street. This takes you into the heart of Temple Bar where the streets come alive after dark and live music fills the air of its legendary traditional pubs.

CONTENTS

A NOTE TO READERS

At Rough Guides, we always strive to bring you the most up-to-date information. This book was produced during a period of continuing uncertainty caused by the Covid-19 pandemic, so please note that content is more subject to change than usual. We recommend checking the latest restrictions and official guidance.

OVERVIEW

Dublin is a fast-paced, youthful city – Ireland has the youngest population in Europe – and is home to over a quarter of the country's total population. The city pulsates with culture, creativity, and history. At night, Dublin's streets are lively with revellers who pour into the city's pubs, bars, clubs, and theatres. By day, people throng the popular shopping streets, cafés, restaurants, galleries, and museums.

The city's character is infused with both Irish charm, proverbial Irish hospitality has not been lost in Dublin's increasing bustle, and European sophistication. The fusion of Irish and international, is celebrated in Dublin's spectacular modern architecture; the sleek harp-like Samuel Beckett Bridge, designed by Spanish architect Santiago Calatrava in conjunction with Dublin engineering firm Roughan O'Donovan; and Daniel Libeskind's Grand Canal Theatre, the beating heart of the regenerated Docklands area.

Dublin sits on over a thousand years of history; the city's roots are in fourth century *Áth Cliath* (Hurdled Ford), seventh century monastic *Duiblinn* (Blackpool), ninth century Viking longphuirt and the resultant eleventh century Hiberno-Norse town. Its history is written in its buildings, from the Anglo-Norman walls of the old city; the derelict Georgian mansions of Henrietta Street; to the bullet holes riddling the General Post Office.

If one foot is in the past, the other is firmly in the present – Dublin has evolved its own new culture, infused with the international influences of its immigrant communities, and claimed a seat at the table of cutting-edge European art, design, and music.

Beyond the bars and displays of lurid green leprechauns and kitsch souvenirs, are the cobbled lanes and galleries of Temple Bar. The works on display show off a clutch of dynamic artists, and photographers, whose talent has looked to the world stage. In the boutiques of the Creative Quarter, designers have made high fashion out of hand knits and tweeds, and given home furnishings a new identity. Dublin's musicians have long since proven that you no longer need a *bodhrán* (an Irish drum) to make it in Irish music.

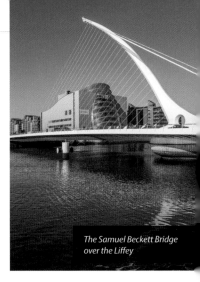

The Samuel Beckett Bridge over the Liffey

With renewal comes restoration. The boom years up to 2008 brought with them a new emphasis on historic preservation. Within the city limits you can view artefacts from the Bronze Age, trace the history of the Easter Rising, or recreate Leopold Bloom's odyssey in *Ulysses*.

CITY ON THE LIFFEY

The River Liffey rises in the Wicklow Mountains and flows from west to east through the centre of the city – north and south are linked by a series of bridges – to Dublin Bay. Historically, the river has cut a social and economic divide between the middle-class southside and working-class north; the latter often promoted as the only 'real' Dublin. Tactfully the new Docklands development spans both banks of the river.

To the north and south are the sweeping curves of the Royal and Grand Canals. The occasional cry of gulls and unexpected distant vista, will remind you that Dublin is a city on the sea, and that the Wicklow Mountains hold it close to the coast.

Dublin is a compact city, physically small and tightly packed, making it a perfect place for walking. College Green, the home of Trinity College, provides a focal point just south of O'Connell Bridge. O'Connell Street, the city's grand boulevard, leads north to Parnell Square and the Garden of Remembrance. To the southeast is St Stephen's Green, the largest of the city's five Georgian squares. To the west, along the south bank of the Liffey, is Temple Bar. Uphill from there lie Dublin Castle and Christ Church Cathedral.

ENJOYING DUBLIN

Literature has always flourished in Dublin, the city has produced three Nobel Prize–winning writers – Yeats, Shaw, and Beckett. In 2010, Dublin became the world's fourth UNESCO City of Literature. Joyce, the high priest of literary Modernism, imagined and interpreted Dublin for the world in *Ulysses*. You will find references to Joyce's work throughout the city.

Dublin theatre is legendary. No visitor should miss seeing a performance at the Abbey or Gate theatres. The city's impact on the rock and pop music scene with the likes of Thin Lizzy, U2, and Boyzone is well known but it continues too, with the emergence of artists and bands like David Balfe, Damien Rice, the Fontaines DC, and Murder Capital. Traditional Irish music is alive and well, especially in the pubs. There has been a revival of storytelling, poetry reading, and traditional dancing. Visual arts are showcased

Lighting conditions

It won't rain on you in Dublin all the time. The climate here can best be described as 'changeable', and yet the sudden shifts from light to dark, sunshine to shower, are part of the city's magic. Buildings seem to transform themselves depending on the light; Dublin under a glowering sky is a very different place from Dublin in the sunshine.

at the Museum of Modern Art in Kilmainham and places like the Project Arts Centre in the heart of Temple Bar.

Grafton Street is the chic place to shop, but retailers all over the city carry an array of goods, as well as Irish crafts and souvenirs. The city is packed with locally owned boutiques and colourful delis. Many shops, hotels, and guesthouses have been owned and managed by the same families for years, and theirs

Performing in a Temple Bar pub

is the welcome of traditional Dublin hospitality.

CITY AND COUNTRYSIDE

Phoenix Park in the northwest is one of the largest city parks in Europe, and is home to Dublin Zoo. There are green pockets throughout the city and its environs; St Stephen's Green Park, Merrion Square, Iveagh Gardens, and the lush Botanic Gardens among others.

On the coast, Seapoint Beach, Portmarnock Beach, and Killiney Beach are the places to go for a blast of sea air. All three have been awarded a Blue Flag. In 1981, UNESCO designated North Bull Island as a Biosphere due to its rare habitats and wildlife. In 2015, this was expanded, to encompass Dublin Bay, North Bull Island and neighbouring land.

The Dublin Mountains are 13km (8 miles) south of the city centre and offer a host of scenic trails. There are walks to suit all skill and fitness levels.

HISTORY AND CULTURE

Inhabited since at least the Mesolithic period. Prehistoric Ireland was shaped by successive waves of mass migration; over the span of millennia new settlers supplanted the early semi-nomadic-hunter-fisher-gathers; introducing agriculture, pottery, religions, funerary rites, metalworking, and a new Goidelic language – the foundations for a civilisation.

The Celts were organised into a clan system, and Celtic Ireland became a series of independent kingdoms. These kingdoms acknowledged an elected high king as overlord, with his seat at fabled Tara. There were no towns and livestock were the medium of exchange. Learning was revered, games were played, and the poet was held in awe. Law and religion were important in Celtic culture. The religion was druidic, and the law was an elaborate written code, interpreted by a class of professional lawyers known as *brehons*. The *brehon* laws gave women a high status – they could own property, divorce, and even enter a profession.

CHRISTIANITY AND A MISSION TO EUROPE

St Patrick first came to Ireland as a slave – captured in an Irish raid on a Romano-British settlement. He eventually escaped, but returned to Ireland as a missionary in AD 432. By the time of his death in AD 465, the whole country had been peacefully Christianised. It was St Patrick who apparently used the example of the shamrock to explain the Christian Trinity to King Laoghaire and an assembled crowd at Tara. The king was converted and the plant has been a symbol of Ireland ever since.

With Christianity and the sophisticated Celtic culture successfully fused, Ireland entered its 'Golden Age' (AD 500 until around AD 800). Ireland's monasteries became major preserves of learning and literacy in the so-called 'Dark Ages'. Ireland was 'the light of the known world', sending its saints and scholars across Europe as part of the Hiberno-Scottish mission.

THE VIKINGS ARRIVE

Throughout this period, Ireland's political organisation continued much as it had under pagan rule. There were still no large towns; the site of present-day Dublin was only a crossroads between two small settlements: *Átha Cliath* (Hurdled Ford), the Irish name that is still omnipresent on road signs and buses, and *Duiblinn* (Blackpool), which eventually gave the city its name. From AD 795, the Vikings repeatedly raided Ireland, sacking the great centres of learning. In the ninth century, the Norse established longphuirt on the Liffey and founded Ireland's first town, which evolved into modern Dublin. The remains of Viking fortifi-cations can be seen today beneath Dublin Castle. The Vikings also introduced coin-age and better shipbuilding techniques.

In AD 988 the Irish kings finally united under the King of Munster, Brian Ború, and drove the Vikings north of the Liffey. After this defeat the Viking influence waned, and they began to be absorbed into the general population, becoming Hiberno-Norse. The Irish claimed Dublin and in 1038 the first Christ Church Cathedral was founded.

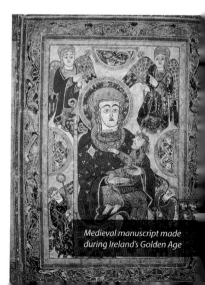

Medieval manuscript made during Ireland's Golden Age

ENGLISH RULE BEGINS

In 1169, Normans landed in Wexford to aid the deposed king of Leinster, Dermot Macmurrough, reclaim his kingdom. Led by Strongbow, the main army arrived at Passage East in 1170 and took Waterford. They reunited with the advance party and Dermot and marched on Dublin; beginning the struggle between England and Ireland that would dominate Irish history. Strongbow married Dermot's daughter Aoife, and when Dermot died in 1171, claimed the kingdom of Leinster. Alarmed by this development, King Henry II arrived that winter with a vast army to assert control over his vassal. The Treaty of Windsor (1175) recognised Ruaidrí's Ua Conchobair's – king of Connacht and high-king of Ireland – kingship over territories outside Norman control, but this proved toothless; by the end of the century two-thirds of Ireland was under Norman control and an age of feudalism had begun.

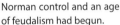

BEYOND THE PALE

The Anglo-Normans became rapidly assimilated, following the pattern of earlier invaders. However, the next two centuries were characterised by repeated attempts by the Irish to rid themselves of their overlords. They were very nearly successful: by the end of the fifteenth century, England held only a small area known as 'the Pale' around Norman Dublin. A fortified

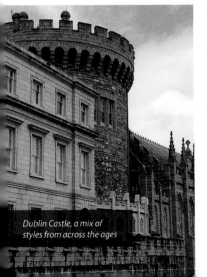

Dublin Castle, a mix of styles from across the ages

ditch was constructed in certain areas to protect the now diminutive Norman holdings from the 'wild Irish' controlling the countryside beyond.

This changed under the Tudor monarchs Henry VIII and Elizabeth I, who were determined to subdue Ireland. Henry VIII's break with Rome and the Dissolution of the Monasteries meant that by 1558 Dublin's two cathedrals, St Patrick's and Christ Church, had become Protestant (they remain so today). Elizabeth I founded Trinity College in Dublin as a seat of Protestant learning, and it remained just that well into the twentieth century. From the mid–sixteenth century, the plantation system saw the best farmland confiscated from Catholics and given to Protestant settlers.

The Irish continued to resist, but the semi-independent kingdoms were never able to achieve real cohesion. In 1607, they were left leaderless when O'Neill and O'Donnell went into exile – known as the 'Flight of the Earls' – clearing the way for James I's Ulster plantations.

FROM CROMWELL TO THE BOYNE

In 1649, Ireland's most hated conqueror, Oliver Cromwell – Lord Protector of Ireland – arrived in Dublin, determined to quash the Irish rebellion. His, and the brutal campaigns of his successors resulted in more than 600,000 Irish dead or deported. There was a massive dispossession of the Irish from their fertile lands in the east, and they were driven west of the Shannon. In Cromwell's own turn-of-phrase they could go 'To Hell or to Connaught'. Some Irish still grimace when they hear his name.

At the end of the century when the Catholic king James II came to the throne, the Irish felt they had no choice but to back him. James was defeated by William of Orange just north of Dublin at the Battle of the Boyne in 1690. As a result, the English parliament enacted the Penal Laws of 1704, which disenfranchised Catholics, keeping the majority of Irish poor and powerless.

Wolfe Tone

GRATTAN AND WOLFE TONE

During the eighteenth century the political, economic, and social domination of the elite Protestant Ascendancy flourished. Ireland's new leaders had come to identify themselves as Irish, and aspired to achieve a measure of self-government for Ireland. It was largely through the energies of Henry Grattan, MP for the city, that England granted legislative independence for Ireland in 1783. Grattan also succeeded in having most of the Penal Laws repealed. However, the independent parliament was short-lived. Against Grattan's opposition, and through bribery and corruption, it voted to dissolve itself in 1800.

Meanwhile, the influential ideas of the French Revolution were spreading. The United Irishmen, led by Wolfe Tone, was founded in 1791 – a non-sectarian movement that sought the freedom of the Irish people, both Catholic and Protestant. Wolfe Tone secured aid from France, but a storm scattered the ships of the invading force. Tone was captured and committed suicide before he could be hanged. He remains a revered figure in the Irish pantheon.

THE UNION AND O'CONNELL

The 1801 Act of Union vastly reduced Dublin's significance as a European city. With the Irish parliament dissolved, MPs had to travel to London to sit at Westminster. In 1803, the great Irish hero

Robert Emmet led yet another failed rebellion. His speech from the dock and his horrendous execution became legendary. Daniel O'Connell carried on the struggle. He believed that the fight for freedom should be fought politically and formed the peaceful but powerful Catholic Association. In 1829, the Duke of Wellington, in a bid to avoid a civil war, passed the Catholic Emanzcipation Bill, allowing Irish Catholics to sit in the parliament at Westminster for the first time. O'Connell was made Lord Mayor of Dublin in 1841, but failed in his bid to have the Act of Union repealed and an Irish parliament re-established.

FAMINE AND HOME RULE

The Great Famine struck in 1845, with a blight on the potato, the staple food of the poor. The crop completely failed for several successive years. It is estimated that more than one million people died and as many emigrated to escape the ravages of the catastrophe. By the end of the century Ireland's population had almost halved. There was plenty of food – corn, cattle, sheep, and flour – but it wasn't available to the poor, and was still being transported to Britain, an outrage that has fed the nationalist cause ever since.

The mid-1900s saw a rise in nationalism. In 1858, the Republican Brotherhood (IRB) was founded in Dublin; and the Fenian Brotherhood in America. Michael Davitt founded the National Land League in 1879 to protest unfair rent, taxes, and evictions. His cause was taken up by Irish MP, Charles Stewart Parnell, and the Land Act passed in 1881. Parnell then turned to the restoration of parliament. A Home Rule Bill was put to the vote in 1886 but was defeated by thirty votes. In 1889, Parnell was involved in a scandalous divorce case, and was replaced as leader of the Home Rule party. The second Home Rule Bill (1893) also failed. In 1912, a third attempt was made but with the outbreak of the First World War it was left in limbo.

James Connolly

THE FIGHT FOR FREEDOM

On Easter Monday, 1916, around 1,500 armed nationalists, led by Thomas J. Clarke, Sean MacDiarmada, Padraig Pearse, James Connolly, Thomas MacDonagh, Eamonn Ceannt, and Joseph Plunkett seized control of six buildings across the capital. Pearse read the Proclamation of the Irish Republic from the General Post Office (GPO) on O'Connell Street. After six days of fighting 'to prevent further slaughter' Pearse declared an unconditional surrender. Nearly five hundred people had been killed – over half were civilians. The brutality of the British retribution turned public opinion in favour of the insurgents. The execution of sixteen prominent insurgents – Connolly was brought to his execution in an ambulance and shot while tied to a chair – caused outrage. In the words of Yeats: 'All changed, changed utterly, a terrible beauty is born' – the Irish wanted full independence.

In the aftermath of the 1916 Rising, Republicans swarmed to Arthur Griffin's Sein Féin party (Ourselves). In the general election of

1919, Sinn Féin won an overwhelming number of the votes. Instead of going to London, they set up a rebel parliament – the first Dáil Éireann – sparking the War of Independence. The war ended in 1921 with the signing of The Anglo-Irish Treaty; this conferred a dominion status, and provision of a Boundary Commission for Northern Ireland if they choose to opt out of the new state. Ireland was partitioned on 3 May 1921. In April 1922, civil war broke out between the supporters of Michael Collins and Arthur Griffith, who'd signed the treaty, and Éamon de Valera's followers who had rejected it. It was a short, bitter conflict; a ceasefire was called and the war ended in May 1923.

INDEPENDENCE AND AFTER

In 1937, de Valera drew up a new constitution that asserted Ireland's sovereignty and claimed political jurisdiction over the whole of Ireland. It also gave the state the new name Éire and created the office of President of Ireland. The country elected its first president, Douglas Hyde, in 1938. During the Second World War, although

GEORGIAN DUBLIN

The Ascendancy in Dublin enjoyed an elegant lifestyle during this period. Theatre and music flourished. Dublin's importance grew dramatically as the city became the centre of social and business life in Ireland. Craftsmen and architects were imported from Europe and England to create public buildings such as the Custom House and the Four Courts; private mansions like Powerscourt and Leinster House; and Georgian squares like Merrion Square in south Dublin.

The glory of this lively and cosmopolitan city lasted until 1801, when the Act of Union brought Ireland under direct rule from London. Suddenly, everything stagnated. The rich and powerful left for England, and the city became a provincial capital in a state of long, slow decline.

The Irish flag flying over the General Post Office

German bombs fell twice on Dublin, the country remained neutral. In 1949, Ireland officially left the Commonwealth and became the Republic of Ireland. 1950s Ireland is synonymous with austerity, mass migration, political instability, and the Catholic Church.

In the late 1960s violence between Catholics and Protestants flared up in Northern Ireland. Riots broke out and the British Army was called in to restore order. This marked the beginning of what is known as 'the Troubles' and the emergence of the Civil Rights movement.

In 1973, Ireland joined the European Economic Community (EEC, later EU) and by the 1990s the 'Celtic Tiger' economy was roaring. In 1990, Mary Robinson was elected Ireland's first woman president, and the Catholic Church's influence began to wane. A ceasefire is called in Northern Ireland in 1997, and the Good Friday Peace Agreement was signed in 1998, ending three decades of sectarian violence.

In 2002, Ireland adopted the euro and the economy soared, only to crash spectacularly in 2008. By 2014 it had largely recovered and the country was seen to be continuously progressive in its outlook, legalising gay marriage in 2015 and decriminalising abortion in 2018. While the UK's vote to leave the EU in 2016 sent shockwaves through the country; followed by the mass disruption of the Covid-19 pandemic in 2020, the economy stands firm. In 2021 the Irish population topped five million for the first time since the Great Famine of the 1800s.

IMPORTANT DATES

8000BC First evidence of human habitation in Ireland.
AD432 St Patrick brings Christianity to Ireland.
AD795 The Vikings arrive.
1038 Christ Church established.
1171 Henry II lands at Dublin and claims feudal lordship.
1204 Anglo-Normans rule from Dublin Castle.
1297 First parliamentary sessions in Dublin.
1592 Founding of Trinity College by Elizabeth I.
1649 Oliver Cromwell invades Ireland and devastates the country.
1690 Supporters of James II defeated at the Battle of the Boyne.
1791 Wolfe Tone's rebellion.
1800–01 The Irish Parliament dissolved.
1803 Robert Emmet's rebellion and execution.
1829 Daniel O'Connell gets the Catholic Emancipation Act passed.
1845-1849 The Great Famine.
1916 The Easter Rising.
1919 Sinn Féin forms the first Dáil and declares Irish independence.
1919–21 War of Independence. Creation of the Irish Free State.
1922–23 The Irish Civil War.
1937 Irish constitution adopted. Irish Free State is renamed Éire.
1949 Ireland becomes a republic.
1973 Ireland joins the European Economic Community (EEC, later EU).
2008 Ireland's economic boom turns into recession.
2015 Ireland legalises same-sex marriage.
2016 Britain votes to leave the EU.
2017 Enda Kenny resigns and Leo Varadkar becomes Taoiseach.
2018 The Republic legalises abortion. President Higgins is re-elected.
2019 Abortion is decriminalised and same-sex marriage is legalised in NI.
2020 First confirmed case of coronavirus in Ireland announced in February. Ireland goes into full lockdown in March.
2021 Irish (Republic) population tops five million for first time since The Great Famine. Ireland Covid-19 vaccination uptake is one of the highest in Europe.

The Custom House

OUT AND ABOUT

Dublin is a compact city, and many of its major attractions are an easy walk from each other. For sightseeing outside the city centre, you can use the capital's buses, trams, and trains or cycle – Dublin City Council runs a self-service bike rental scheme with NOW dublinbikes (www.dublinbikes.ie). For information on Dublin's public transport visit www.transportforireland.ie. The TFI Journey Planner App can be downloaded from Apple App and Google Play stores. Driving is best avoided, as car rental is quite expensive and the city suffers from traffic congestion and a lack of parking.

Your first port of call should be to one of Fáilte Ireland's official tourist offices – Discover Ireland Information Office (14 Upper O'Connell Street; Mon, Tues, Wed, Thurs, Fri & Sat 9am–5pm; www.discoverireland.ie) and the **Visit Dublin Centre** (Mon, Tues, Wed, Thurs, Fri & Sat 9am–5pm; www.visitdublin.com) – for advice, information, maps, and pamphlets. Their offices provide a booking service for accommodation, attractions, events, festivals, and tours.

A good way to get the lay of the land is to take a hop-on hop-off bus tour with DoDublin (59 Upper O'Connell Street; daily 9am–5pm; 30 stops; https://dodublin.ie) or Big Bus Dublin (13 Upper O'Connell Street; daily 9am–5pm; 25 stops; www.bigbustours.com).

The Dublin Pass

The Dublin Pass, available online, is a digital sightseeing pass that gives you entry to over thirty of the city's top tourist attractions. Depending on what attractions you want to see and when you want to see them the pass can be a thrifty option. Visit https://dublinpass.com for more information.

AROUND GRAFTON STREET

Grafton Street is Dublin's main shopping street, a pedestrianised avenue jostling with shoppers and enlivened by street entertainers. Located south of the river, this central thoroughfare is lined with stores including the famous Brown Thomas department store and high-end jeweller Weir & Sons; and the iconic **Bewley's Oriental Café (Mon, Tues, Wed, Thurs & Fri 8.30am–5pm, Sat & Sun 9.30am-6pm)**, notable for its distinctive Art Deco facade and Harry Clarke stained-glass windows. The lunchtime café-theatre serves up a comedic repertoire. Stop by for coffee, culture, and comedy. On the alley alongside is **St Teresa's Church (Mon, Tues, Wed, Thurs & Fri 7am–6.30pm, Sat & Sun 8am–7pm)**, with stained-glass windows by Phyllis Burke and a fine sculpture by John Hogan.

Just beyond Bewley's, a signpost points the way to the Clarendon Street entrance of the smart **Powerscourt Townhouse Centre** (59 South William Street; Mon, Tues, Wed, Thurs, Fri & Sat 10am–6pm, Sun noon–6pm), the centrepiece of Dublin's Creative Quarter. Formerly, the residence of Viscount Powerscourt it was redeveloped as a shopping centre in the 1970s and is now home to a gallery, florist, and an array of cafés,

Grafton Street

bars, and restaurants, fashion, jewellery, and antique stores. The Georgian townhouse has been sympathetically converted and still possesses some magnificent plasterwork, a fine mahogany staircase, and original trompe l'oeil floor.

From South William Street, the Creative Quarter extends to South Great George's Street and from Stephen Street Lower to Exchequer Street. This bohemian area of Dublin – historically, the centre of Dublin's rag trade – encompasses artisan boutiques, studios and galleries, and cafés and restaurants. The bustling **George's Street Arcade** (Mon, Tues & Wed 9am–6pm, Thurs, Fri & Sat 9am–8pm, Sun noon–6pm) runs between Drury Street and South Great George's Street. The arcade is Dublin's first purpose-built shopping centre – it opened in 1881 – and houses over forty independent retailers selling everything from vinyl records to vintage clothing, stamps to speciality foods, and coin collections to costume jewellery.

South Great George's Street reaches north to Dame Street; the junction of Dame Street with College Green is to the east. The Palladian-style Parliament House (now Bank of Ireland; Mon, Tues, Wed, Thurs & Fri 10am–4pm) occupies the north side of College Green. Designed by Sir Edward Lovett Pearce, it was constructed between 1728 and 1739 to house the Irish Parliament. The curved screen wall and the Corinthian portico and the western colonnade and portico are late-eighteenth century additions. The matching curved wall on the west side was added in the 1800s when the building was remodelled for use as a bank. With the exception of the corridor and the House of Lords with its eighteenth-century tapestries and coffered ceiling little of the original interior remains.

TRINITY COLLEGE

Across College Green is **Trinity College** ❶ (www.tcd.ie), founded by Elizabeth I in 1592 to bring Ireland into the fold of European

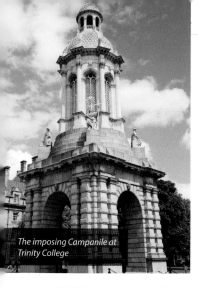

The imposing Campanile at Trinity College

learning. Until the Catholic Relief Act (1793) it was a wholly Protestant institution, and between 1871 and 1970 the Catholic Church forbade Catholics to attend Trinity 'under pain of mortal sin'. Today the college is one of the geographic and social hubs of the city, attracting students from around the world. Famous graduates include Jonathan Swift, Bram Stoker, Oscar Wilde, and Samuel Beckett; nationalist heroes Robert Emmet and Wolfe Tone also studied here.

The university sits on College Green, an island of magnificent buildings, open squares, and green spaces, surrounded by a sea of traffic. You are welcome to explore the campus, but some of the buildings may be closed, depending on the time of year. Walk between the statues of alumni Edmund Burke and Oliver Goldsmith and through the gates of the west front – designed by Theodore Jacobsen and built in 1752 – onto the lawned and cobbled quadrangle, Parliament Square. **The square is flanked** by the Chapel and Dining Hall on the north side and the Public Theatre and 1937 Reading Room on the south side.

The Chapel was created by George III's architect, Sir William Chambers, and erected between 1787 and 1798. The **Chapel** displays some fine plasterwork created by stuccodore Michael Stapleton and dazzling stained-glass windows (installed in 1865, and 1872) together with a twentieth-century organ in an eighteenth-century case. The Dining Hall – completed in 1765 and designed by Hugh Darley – replaced Richard Castle's 1741 structure; a building so unstable it collapsed twice during construction. Misfortune struck for a third time and the Dining Hall was badly damaged in a fire in 1984.

The Public Theatre, built to designs by Chambers from 1777-1786, is rarely open to the public (concerts are occasionally held here) but you can peek through the spy hole in the door. The beautiful elliptical groin vaulted ceiling showcases Stapleton's craftmanship and Robert Home's portraits of Trinity's luminaries adorn the side walls. The 1937 Reading Room, designed by Thomas Manly Deane and named for its year of completion, was conceived as a war memorial library. The Hall of Honour – the entrance to the octagonal reading room - was inaugurated in 1928. In 2015, a memorial stone was laid outside the Hall to commemorate the 471 Trinity staff, students, and alumni who were killed during the First World War.

The Campanile, is the focal point of the first and second quadrangle, Library Square. Built in 1853 by Sir Charles Lanyon, the 30m- (100ft-) high **Campanile** houses the university's bells. Also occupying the square is Henry Moore's sinuous, modernist bronze *Reclining Connected Forms (1969).* Library Square is lined by the Graduates' Memorial Building (GMB) on the north side and the Old Library on the south side. The Gothic Revival GMB, designed by Sir Thomas Drew, was built in 1902 to celebrate the tercentenary of Trinity's founding. Thomas Burgh's imposing three-storey Old Library was erected between 1712 and 1733. The original flat ceiling in the aptly named Long Room – it is 64m- (209ft-) long - was replaced with the current barrel-vaulted ceiling by Deane & Woodward in the 1860s. The Old Library holds Trinity's oldest books, including a Shakespeare folio, but its greatest treasure is the ninth-century Book of Kells.

The Book of Kells (May–Sept daily 9.30am–5pm; Oct–April Mon, Tues, Wed, Thurs, Fri & Sat 9.30am–5pm, Sun noon–4.30pm; www.tcd.ie/visitors/book-of-kells) has been on exhibit in the Old Library since the mid–nineteenth century. It contains the Gospels of Matthew, Mark, Luke, and John – the Gospel of John is incomplete – and is widely acknowledged as a masterpiece of medieval Christian art. In 1953, the folios were bound into four volumes. Two are usually on display, one opened to show a major decorative illustration, and one to reveal two pages of ornamental script.

Behind the Old Library is Fellows' Square, home to Alexander Calder's welded steel sculpture *Cactus* Provisoire (1967). The square is framed by the Brutalist-style **Berkeley Library – built in 1967 by** modernist architect Paul Koralek **- and** the 1970s Arts Building. Housed in the Arts Building is the airy **Douglas Hyde Gallery** (www.douglashydegallery.com; Mon–Fri 11am–6pm, Thurs until 7pm, Sat 11am–5.30pm; free), a modern two-level exhibition space and the place to go for cutting edge Irish and international art.

Trinity celebrated its quatercentenary in 1992 with the opening of the Samuel Beckett Theatre (www.tcd.ie/drama). The Theatre lies off the northeast corner of New Square and showcases original student work. It also hosts national and international dance and theatre companies. Southeast of the Theatre is the teen-friendly Science Gallery Dublin (Wed 11am-6pm, Thurs 11am-7pm, Fri 11am-6pm, Sat & Sun noon-5pm; https://dublin.sciencegallery.com) which merges science, art, technology, and design.

All-in ticket

For an audio tour of the Book of Kells and the Old Library, download the free Visit Trinity app from the Apple App Store or Google Play Store. Concession tickets are available for senior citizens and students with a valid student card. see page 27.

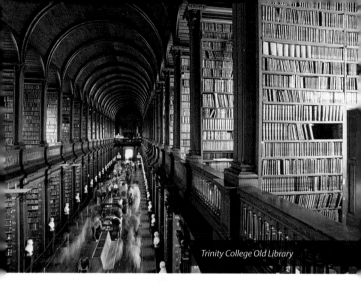

Trinity College Old Library

DAWSON AND KILDARE STREETS

From College Green head along Nassau Street and spend some time browsing its craft and souvenir shops, then turn right onto Dawson Street. Here you will find bookshops, a smattering of upmarket boutiques, and another shopping complex, the **Royal Hibernian Way**.

St Ann's Church (Dawson Street; Wed, Thurs & Fri 11am–2pm) has some colourful Victorian stained glass, and is a popular venue for daytime concerts. A few doors down is the charming **Mansion House**, built between 1705 and 1710 for a property speculator, Joshua Dawson (for whom the street is named). He whimsically sold it to the Dublin Corporation in 1715 for £3,500 and a six-pound loaf of double refined sugar at Christmas; it has been the official residence of the Lord Mayor of Dublin ever since. Behind it is the **Round Room**, where in 1919 the first Dáil (the lower house of parliament) read out the Declaration of Independence.

Leinster House, seat of Ireland's Parliament

Take Molesworth Street (across from the Royal Hibernian Way) to Kildare Street. You will see the elegant entrance to **Leinster House** (tel: 01 618 3271; www.oireachtas.ie/en/visit-and-learn); once the town residence of the earls of Kildare, it is now home to the Irish parliament, and is likely the inspiration for the White House in Washington DC, designed by Irish architect James Hoban.

Leinster House is bookended by 'twin' buildings – **the National Library of Ireland** (Mon, Tues, Wed, Thurs & Fri 9.30am–5pm; tel: 01 603 0200; www.nli.ie), and the National Museum of Ireland – Archaeology – designed by Thomas Newenham Deane and his son Thomas Manly Deane, each features a large rotunda at its core. Tickets are required for the reading room (Readers Ticket Office; 10.30am–12.30pm), which is in the rotunda itself. Over half a million items here provide a vast archive of the nation. Exhibitions are held in the entrance hall and a dedicated basement space. The Family History Research Room is available by appointment. The National

Museum of Ireland – Archaeology ❷ houses important archaeological artefacts dating from the Mesolithic up to the twentieth century. Admission to all National Museum of Ireland sites (Archaeology, Country Life, Decorative Arts & History, and Natural History) is free; however, you must book a ticket in advance of your visit. Opened in 1890, the building itself is noteworthy for its entrance hall and Rotunda, mosaic floors, and the elaborate blue-and-yellow majolica decoration on the pediments and jambs of the doors. The exhibits are state-of-the-art. **Ór: Ireland's Gold** showcases the astonishing accomplishments of goldsmiths from 2200BC to 700BC. Medieval treasures include the Ardagh Chalice, and Tara Brooch, along with metalwork from the Viking period. The museum also has a small Egyptian gallery and an exhibit on the history of Irish independence.

Towards the northern end of street, is the Kildare Street Club (now Alliance Française; National Library of Ireland; 1–3 Kildare Street). This marvellous Victorian-Gothic building – built by Deane & Woodward in 1861 – is famous for the fanciful stone carvings around the base of its pillars. One pillar, reputedly depicting the club members, shows monkeys playing billiards. The club itself was a bastion of Ascendancy establishment. The Library's Department of Manuscripts and the Office of the Chief Herald (if you qualify and have the requisite cash to spare, you can apply for a Grant of Arms) are located in Number 2, and there is a small exhibition space on the ground floor.

ST STEPHEN'S GREEN

Walk to the south end of Kildare Street and you will reach **St Stephen's Green Park ❸**, a 9-hectare (22-acre) park in the heart of the city, surrounded by beautiful buildings. Previously common grazing land, it was first enclosed in 1663, and by the early-eighteenth century was the fashionable place to promenade. The park was relandscaped between 1877 and 1880 to reflect Victorian tastes. A popular and often crowded place, the Green contains expansive formal lawns, ornate gardens, duck ponds, a bandstand, and a children's playground.

Use the Wolfe Tone Entrance, this is located at the northeastern corner of the park, and you'll see Edward Delaney's Wolfe Tone Memorial (1964) and bronze sculpture *Famine* (1967). Walk south east to the opposite side of the park to Josef Wackerle's limestone fountain and bronze sculpture ***Three Fates – a gift from*** Germany to thank the Irish who opened their country to orphaned German children after World War II. Continue north west and you'll pass Marjorie Fitzgibbon's bust of **James Joyce (1982)**. Follow the path round and pass under the triumphal **Fusilier's Arch (1907).**

On your right are the departure point for horse and carriage tours, and a hop-on hop-off bus stop. Cross the road and visit **The Little**

FINDING YOUR ANCESTORS

If you have an Irish last name or Irish ancestry, you may want to join the crowd that comes to Ireland ancestor hunting. Your grandmother's family stories may be the clue – begin at home by collecting family names.

Dublin is a good place to start your search. Try the National Library on Kildare Street, it has a genealogical department on the first floor, with a large collection of genealogical and historical records. The General Register Office (GRO) operates a research facility at Werburgh Street and you can search the indexes to the registers held by GRO. The National Archives on Bishop Street is the official repository for government records and offers a free genealogy advisory service, and the records at the Registry of the Deeds on Henrietta Street date back to 1708. If you know the county, town or village, you can search the appropriate parish registers. Churchyard monuments and gravestones can also be a source of information.

Museum of Dublin (daily 10am–5pm; www.littlemuseum.ie). The museum occupies a three-storey Georgian house on the corner of Dawson Street. It was set up by Dubliners to introduce their city and offers a fascinating insight into the everyday life of Dubliners over the years. The ground floor hosts temporary exhibitions on Dublin themes, while the first-floor front is furnished as a typical mid–twentieth century drawing room. The

Bust of James Joyce at St Stephen's Green

other rooms display numerous curiosities, ranging from a vintage telephone, old tram seats, to a signed U2 album, and a facsimile of James Joyce's death mask. All of the objects were donated by Dubliners to help visitors gain an insight into their city. Standard admission is by guided tour, rich in Dublin wit and informative,

At the south end of Grafton Street is the **St Stephen's Green Shopping Centre (Mon, Tues & Wed 8.30am–7pm, Thurs 8.30am–8pm, Fri & Sat 8.30am–7pm, Sun 11am–6pm)** – a pseudo-Victorian iron-and-glass structure, it was built in the 1980s and is known locally as 'The Wedding Cake'. The centre houses a wide selection of shops as well as a café-restaurant on the top floor, under the glass dome.

Head east along St Stephen's Green and turn right on to York Street, the **Royal College of Surgeons (RCSI) is unmissable.** Built around 1805 by Edward Parke, it was enlarged by four bays in the 1820s, and is seven bays wide. The chips in the stonework are

Gardeners tending the Green

bullet holes – a simple plaque on the wall identifies the RCSI as the 1916 headquarters of the Irish Citizens Army.

One of Dublin's best-kept secrets is the **Iveagh Gardens (Mon, Tues, Wed, Thurs, Fri & Sat 8am opening, Sun 10am opening)**; walk back up York Street and turn right on to Stephen's Green, and continue on to Harcourt Street. Turn left on to Clonmel Street and veer right when the street forks – the entrance isn't obvious, hence the gardens' sense of seclusion. The gardens can also be accessed from behind the National Concert Hall on Earlsfort Terrace. Designed as a series of pleasure gardens in the Italianate style in 1863 – with cascades, spectacular fountains, and rustic grottoes. Retrace your steps to Harcourt Street and turn left. Number 60 and 61, now part of the Harcourt Hotel, were once home to playwright George Bernard Shaw. From here it is a short walk, following the signs, to the small **Irish-Jewish Museum** (Sept–April Sun 10.30am–2.30pm; May–Sept Sun. Mon, Tues, Wed & Thurs

11am–3pm; www.jewishmuseum.ie) in Walworth Road. This former synagogue tells the story of the Jews in Ireland by means of documents, memorabilia, and old photographs. Set in the heart of what was the city's Jewish quarter in the late–nineteenth and early–twentieth century, it reveals a little-known part of Dublin's community. Look for a Guinness bottle with a Hebrew label.

Back along the south side of St Stephen's Green, you'll find the Romanesque **University Church** tucked between number 87 and number 88; it was constructed in the garden beside and behind number 87 between 1855 and 1856 by Cardinal Henry Newman, the rector of the Catholic University of Ireland – the precursor of University College Dublin (UCD). The small entrance porch conceals a unique and strangely compelling Byzantine-style interior; it is a very popular venue for weddings. Number 85 and number 86, comprise the exquisite UCD **Newman House ❹**. Number 85 was built in 1738 and designed by Richard Castle. It contains the famous Apollo Room, which has panels depicting Apollo and the muses; and a magnificent Rococo salon. The superb stucco is by the Lafranchini brothers, who also worked on Russborough House (see page 75). It's Palazzo-style neighbour was built around 1765 and designed by Robert West and has even more elaborate ornamentation. UCD Newman House has a rich literary heritage – the poet Gerard Manley Hopkins lived here while Professor of Classics at the university and James Joyce and Flann O'Brien were students here. The Museum of Literature Ireland (MoLI; Tues, Wed, Thurs, Fri, Sat & Sun 10.30am–6pm; https://moli.ie/), housed in the Aula Maxima, formerly, the university's assembly hall, completes the complex. In collaboration with the National Library of Ireland, MoLI brings the library's Joyce collections to Joyce's alma mater. The museum pays homage to centuries of Irish storytelling, with exhibits of literary archives and manuscripts, readings, and other events. MoLI also offers a guided tour of UCD Newman House.

Just beyond UCD Newman House is **Iveagh House**, home to the Irish government's Department of Foreign Affairs, however, this is closed to the public.

Beyond Iveagh House in Earlsfort Terrace (turn south) is the **National Concert Hall** (www.nch.ie), of impressive proportions and uncertain acoustics – it is a conversion of an old Examination Hall of University College.

Back at the northeast corner of St Stephen's Green, near the Shelbourne Hotel, you can turn right onto Merrion Row to peer through the railings at the small **Huguenot Cemetery** (no entry to visitors). The cemetery dates back to 1693 when French Protestants fleeing persecution in their native land settled in Dublin. They brought with them their architectural and weaving skills, which greatly enriched their adopted city.

At the end of Ely Place, which runs south from Merrion Row and Baggot Street, is the **Royal Hibernian Academy** (RHA; Mon & Tues 11am–5pm, Wed 11am–6.30pm, Fri & Sat 11am–5pm, Sun noon–5pm; www.rhagallery.ie).

OLD DUBLIN

West of O'Connell Street, between Dublin Castle and Christ Church Cathedral, is the site of the original town of Duiblinn (Blackpool). The Viking settlement spread eastwards along the river towards Trinity College. In 1592, when Trinity was built, the university was in Baile Átha Cliath ('Town of the Hurdled Ford'), which was not in, but near Dublin. The two have now merged.

TEMPLE BAR

Between the river and Dame Street is **Temple Bar** ❺, once a run-down area but now a firm tourism fixture, famous for its nightlife and street action. The narrow, partly pedestrianised,

Newman House contains Rococo busts of man and beast

eighteenth-century cobbled lanes feature some original architecture. The core of Temple Bar can be found in the area between the Central Bank and Merchant's Arch. The area now consists of government-funded arts centres and tourist-oriented shops, with some lively restaurants and bars. The design-led crafts and workshops that originally gave the area its vibrant character have moved east across Parliament Street, and can be found in the Cow's Lane area between Dublin Castle and Essex Quay. Check it out on a Saturday morning when there is a thriving street market for food, books, and designer goods.

You can enter Temple Bar from Dame Street, Fleet Street (off Westmoreland Street), or you can walk through **Merchants Arch**, opposite the picturesque arching Ha'penny Bridge, into Temple Bar Square. Continuing along Temple Bar, you will come to Eustace Street and Meeting House Square. Most of the cultural centres that make Temple Bar interesting are located in this area. The **Irish Film**

Institute Ⓐ (www.irishfilm.ie) in Eustace Street is the main outlet for arthouse and foreign films. It maintains a popular café/bar and its shop has a good selection of posters and books on film theory. Also in Eustace Street is an information office and a culture, arts, and entertainment centre for children, **The Ark Ⓑ** (see page 98) (www.ark.ie).

On Meeting House Square you'll find the **Gallery of Photography (Wed, Thurs, Fri & Sat 11am–6pm; Ⓒ** www.galleryofphotography.ie), which displays photographs of Dublin past and present alongside Irish and international photography exhibitions. There are also books and posters for sale. The **National Photographic Archive Ⓓ** (daily 10am–4pm; www.nli.ie) is also located on Meeting House Square, it maintains the photographic collections of the National Library of Ireland. There are reading rooms for research and temporary exhibitions.

The **Project Arts Centre** (39 East Essex Street; www.projectartscentre.ie) displays avant-garde painting and sculpture and also has a theatre upstairs. **The Button Factory** (www.buttonfactory.ie) nightclub and concert venue is also in the area, as well as **Jam Art Factory** (www.jamartfactory.com), an excellent Irish art and design shop.

On Dame Street, Temple Bar's southern boundary, is a gem of Victorian architecture: the **Olympia Theatre Ⓔ** (www.olympia.ie). Built in 1870, its canopy of stained glass and cast iron is the oldest in Dublin, and its enthusiastic interior decoration is also typical of the era. The restored theatre has a regular schedule of light-hearted plays and concerts. Just across the way is **City Hall** (Mon, Tues, Wed, Thurs, Fri & Sat 10am–5pm; www.dublincity.ie), originally built as the Royal Exchange in 1769–79. Thomas Cooley designed this fine building's Corinthian portico. Just to the west of City Hall lies one of Dublin's most important historic sites, Dublin Castle.

DUBLIN CASTLE

Today, as you walk through the Great Gate into the spacious Georgian yard, **Dublin Castle** ❻ (daily 9.45am–5.45pm; www.dublincastle.ie) looks both serene and imposing. For seven centuries the castle was the real and symbolic centre of British military and social power; it still has resonance for Dubliners today. The castle has been built and rebuilt several times over the course of its history, and little remains of the original Anglo-Norman structure that was built in 1204. It sits on the site of the Duiblinn (Blackpool) that gave Dublin its name. The Viking Excavation and Chapel Royal can only be accessed as part of a guided tour.

The guided tour commences with the **State Apartments** on the south side of the building. Lavishly furnished and decorated, with much original period furniture, the rooms are used for ceremonial

At the heart of Temple Bar

Taking a break outside Dublin Castle

events, visits from foreign dignitaries, and EU meetings. The **Connolly Room** is so-called because it was here that the wounded James Connolly spent his last night before being executed for his part in the Easter Rising. Note the exquisite 'Hibernia Ceiling' in the **Apollo Room;** it was moved here from Mespil House. The Drawing Room was partially destroyed by fire in 1941, so its furnishings are faithful reproductions; the huge (repaired) Ming punch bowl is particularly striking.

A splendid carpet, with a design based on a page from the Book of Kells (see page 30), covers the floor of the **Throne Room**. In 1911, George V was the last to use the rather large throne. In the lovely **Picture Gallery**, convex wall mirrors made it possible for the host at table to keep his eye on everyone, particularly the servants. The enormous **St Patrick's Hall**, with its painted ceiling by Vincenzo Valdre, contains the banners and coats of arms of the now-defunct Knights of St Patrick. The hall is now used for the inauguration of the Irish president.

One of the most interesting parts of the tour is the excavation of the **Viking and Norman Defences**. Visitors can stand in the dry bed of the old moat, traverse imaginative gangways over the encroaching river (the Poddle, not the Liffey), and view the stairs at which boats once landed provisions for the castle. In the restored **Treasury** – built in 1715 and located in the Lower Yard –, browse in the bookshop or relax in the Vaults Restaurant.

The oldest part of the castle is the **Record Tower** (1258). The neo-Gothic **Church of the Most Holy Trinity**, adjacent to the tower, has stone work by Edward Smyth and a fan-vaulted ceiling. The Crypt Theatre is under the church and presents exhibitions, plays, and concerts.

A modern addition to the castle precinct is the award-winning **Chester Beatty Library** ❼ (Tues 9.45am–5.30pm, Wed 9.45am–8pm, Thurs, Fri & Sat 9.45am–5.30pm, Sun noon–5.30pm; www.cbl.ie). The library is a treasure house of Islamic manuscripts, Chinese, Japanese, and Indian, art and texts. Biblical papyri and Christian manuscripts are also on display, completing one of the richest collections of the written word in Western and Eastern cultures. The library itself includes copies of the Koran and codices dating from the second century BC. The gallery's marvellous Silk Road Café provides a menu to match the cultures of the displays.

CHRIST CHURCH CATHEDRAL AND ENVIRONS

Further up the hill on Castle Street from the Great Gate is the first of Dublin's two major cathedrals, **Christ Church Cathedral** ❽ (Mon 10am–5pm, Thurs, Fri & Sat 10am–5pm, Sun 1–3pm; www.christchurchcathedral.ie) in Christchurch Place. Like the castle, the cathedral stands on a hill, rising on the site of Sitric's – the Norse

THE LEGEND OF BRITISH JUSTICE

Above the main gate of Dublin Castle stands a statue of Justice. With its back turned to the city, it was an apt symbol of British rule. The farce does not end there. This Justice, thanks to the naivety of the sculptor, has no blindfold. Furthermore, the statue, inadvertently of course, drained rainwater from the head, down the arm and into the metal scales she holds, tipping them out of balance.

king of Dublin – eleventh-century wooden church. The foundations date to 1172 when Strongbow, the Earl of Pembroke, had it rebuilt as a stone structure. By 1558, after Henry VIII's break with the Roman Catholic Church, all the existing foundations in Dublin had become Anglican.

Unfortunately, the church building was massively and unsympathetically restored in 1871–78 – most of the original interior was ripped out. However, there is still much to appreciate in Christ Church, including the impressive stonework, soaring nave, and the handsome nineteenth-century encaustic floor tiles based on a thirteenth-century pattern. Strongbow's tomb is in the church; while in the **Peace Chapel** is a somewhat macabre artefact – the embalmed heart of St Laurence O'Toole (the influential twelfth-century archbishop of Dublin) is kept in a cage suspended on the

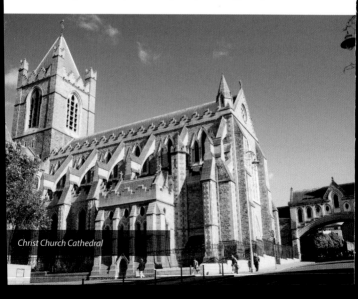

Christ Church Cathedral

wall near the altar. The cathedral choir traces its origins back to 1480 and has the distinction of taking part in the world's first ever performance of Handel's Messiah. Choral Evensong is on Sundays, Tuesdays, Wednesdays, and Thursdays at 6pm.

The vast, vaulted medieval crypt is the oldest structure in Dublin. An exhibition, entitled **Treasures of Christ Church**, takes up much of the crypt. An additional charge is required to see this limited number of ancient texts, plus the tabernacle of James II, a William of Orange plate, commemorating his victory in the Battle of the Boyne, and a 1666 Common Prayer Book. A few items of note are in the open areas of the crypt, among the forest of heavy stone pillars. These include stocks dating from 1670, medieval carved stones, and a curious exhibit – a mummified cat and a rat, found trapped in the organ pipes.

In the Old Synod Hall, just across the road from the cathedral (and linked to it by a bridge), you will find **Dublinia** ❾ (Thurs, Fri, Sat & Sun 10am–5.30pm; www.dublinia.ie). This impressive rec-reation of Dublin in medieval times incorporates state-of-the-art interactive exhibits and reconstructions to enhance the sights, sounds, and even the smells of the city. Exhibitions include an archaeological lab and excavation site, life on board a Viking war-ship, burial customs, and the looting of monasteries. You can also climb St Michael's Tower for a view over the city.

Wood Quay, on the south bank of the river is the site of a Viking settlement. It stands downhill from the arch and is domi-nated by the offices of the Dublin Corporation. The construction of these offices obliterated much of the archaeological dig that unearthed the original layout of the ninth-century quay, but the artefacts that were found are on view in the National Museum (see page 32).

A short distance from the cathedral on High Street are the two **St Audoen's churches**. The restored Church of Ireland St

Exhibit at Dublinia

Audoen's is the older of the two (1190) and is the only remaining medieval church in the city. Next door is the narrow, lofty, neo-classical facade of Catholic St Audoen's, built in 1847. Both churches stand beside what remains of the old city walls, and St Audoen's is the only surviving gate. In medieval times, the High Cross of the Norman city – where decrees and notices of excommunication were read out – stood on the High Street. Granite markers erected in 1991 indicate the line of the old city walls.

West from here on Thomas Street, a plaque on the wall of **St Catherine's Church** (built between 1760 and 1769) marks the spot where the revered Irish revolutionary Robert Emmet was hanged in 1803. **John's Lane Church** further down Thomas Street is more remarkable. Though just over 100 years old, it is one of the most attractive churches in the city. Thomas Street West becomes James's Street, where the **Guinness Brewery** has been situated ever since 1759.

GUINNESS BREWERY AND BEYOND

Well west of the city centre lie several of Dublin's top tourist attractions. Handily, they are all clustered near Heuston Station, which is well serviced by buses and trams. The **Guinness Storehouse** 🔟 (Sun, Mon, Tues, Wed & Thurs 10am–5pm, Sat & Sun 10am–7pm;

www.guinness-storehouse.com) is the latest incarnation of the Guinness Brewery tour and an ultramodern one at that. This self-guided tour begins on the ground level with ingredients, and ends in the very stylish **Gravity Bar** atop the brewery with a 360-degree view of Dublin. Adult ticket prices include a pint of Guinness (under eighteens get a soft drink). Along the way you get to see and sniff the various stages of the brewing process. Despite all the entertaining technology, the tour is ultimately educational, as you watch films of old coopers making the casks for the brew, and learn just how Guinness is created from the four simple ingredients of water, barley, hops, and yeast.

The restored Royal Hospital at Kilmainham, which now houses the **Irish Museum of Modern Art** ⓫ (Tues 10am–5.30pm, Wed 11.30am–5.30pm, Thurs, Fri & Sat 10am–5.30pm, Sun

Going with the flow at the Guinness Storehouse

noon–5.30pm www.imma.ie) is Dublin's most important seventeenth-century building (1684). With its wonderful light and space, it makes a tremendous exhibition area. The museum's holdings include the Gordon Lambert Collection, with more than one hundred works dating from the 1960s and 1970s. However, the real attractions are the numerous temporary exhibits. There is an international residency programme for artists, and visitors may meet the artists in their studios (depending on schedules). Concerts and special events are also held in the museum, and there is an atmospheric café in the vaults. A good range of contemporary art books, posters, and postcards can be found in the gallery bookshop.

Further west is the evocative museum of the **Kilmainham Gaol** ⑫ (Oct–Mar 9.30am–5.30pm; April–May 9am–6pm; June–Sept 9.30am–6pm; www.kilmainhamgaolmuseum.ie). Kilmainham was the major Irish prison for well over a century, with prisoners including future taoiseach (prime minister) Éamon de Valera. An excellent exhibition traces the history of the prison, as well as the political and social events that brought many of the prisoners here. Victorian theories about prisons and the treatment of prisoners are explored in one exhibition space. A twenty-five-minute audio-visual presentation in the prison chapel is followed by a guided tour through

Enjoying the view of Dublin from Gravity Bar

the dark corridors of the eighteenth-century part of the building, where you can see the cells the condemned leaders of the Easter Rising occupied – they were executed in the prison yard.

A tour of Kilmainham Gaol

Nearby, on the south bank of the Liffey opposite Phoenix Park, is the **Irish National War Memorial Park.** Created in the 1930s to designs by the architect and landscape designer Edwin Lutyens, the gardens are a tribute to the thousands of Irish soldiers who died in World War I while serving in the British Army. The sombre design incorporates the War Stone and four granite pavilions, one of which contains Celtic and art deco illuminated manuscripts by the book illustrator and stained-glass artist Harry Clarke, listing the names of those killed in action.

On the north bank of the Liffey, behind Wolfe Tone Quay, are the former **Collins Barracks**. Built in 1701, the barracks were occupied continuously until 1997. Since then, they have been home to the **National Museum of Ireland – Decorative Arts and History** ⓭ (Tues, Wed, Thurs, Fri & Sat 10am–5pm, Sun & Mon 1–5pm; www.museum.ie). Silver, ceramics, furniture, and folk artefacts trace Ireland's social and political history. There is also a café and bookshop.

THE LIBERTIES

Back towards the city centre now, and to the south of High Street, the area known as the **Liberties** was so named because it was situated outside the medieval city walls and was run by local courts, free of city regulations on trade. The area, once impoverished, is slowly gentrifying, with new housing and restoration of the original small red-brick houses.

Across from the two St Audoen's (see page 45), two interesting streets run off High Street. Francis Street is lined with antiques shops, full of glittering treasures. In Back Lane you'll find the headquarters of An Taisce (The National Trust for Ireland), an organisation dedicated to the preservation of historic buildings and gardens in Ireland. It is located in the delightful **Tailors' Hall**, the oldest guildhall in Ireland; once used by hosier, tailors, and barbersurgeons' guilds. It dates from 1706, and is one of the few remaining original Queen Anne buildings in Dublin.

ST PATRICK'S CATHEDRAL

At the eastern end of Back Lane and turning right, Nicholas Street becomes Patrick Street. On the left, off St Patrick's Close, is **St Patrick's Cathedral** ⓮ March–Oct Mon, Tues, Wed, Thurs, Fri & Sat 9.30am–5pm, Sun 9–10.30am,   12.30–2.30pm, 4.30–4.30pm; Nov–Feb Mon, Tues, Wed, Thurs & Fri 9.30am–5pm, Sat 9am–5pm, Sun 9–10.30am, 12.30–2.30pm; www.stpatrickscathedral.ie). This is the oldest Christian site in Dublin. St Patrick himself is reputed to have baptised converts on this spot, marked by a Celtic cross in the nave, suggesting that there has been a church here since around AD 450. In the adjoining St Patrick's Park, a marker shows the site of **St Patrick's Well**.

The height and space of the cathedral are impressive. Note the carved helmets and swords set above the choir stalls and the nineteenth-century tiled floor, similar to the one in Christ Church. The 90m- (300ft) interior makes it the longest church in the country. The 45m- (150ft-) high tower holds the largest ringing peal of bells in Ireland. Not much is left of the original construction of 1191.

Destroyed in a fire in the fourteenth century, it was later rebuilt, and even includes some Victorian restoration work.

The cathedral has had a varied history. From 1320, until Henry VIII closed it, St Patrick's was the seat of Ireland's first university. Later, Cromwellian troops used the aisles to stable their horses. The great Jonathan Swift, author of Gulliver's Travels, was dean here from 1713 to 1745. He was much revered for his satirical genius, charity, and championship of the Irish poor. You can see his grave and that of his great love, Esther Johnson, as well as the pulpit from which he preached. On the wall is the epitaph he wrote for himself.

An interesting artefact from the medieval chapter house is a door with a hole in it. Lord Kildare cut the hole in 1492 so he could reassure his archenemy Lord Ormonde, who was under siege in the chapter house, of his friendly intentions. Kildare put his arm

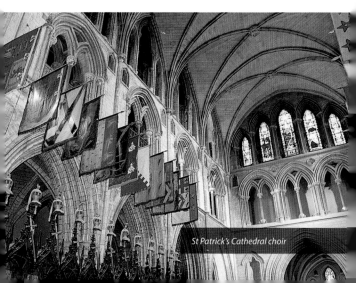

St Patrick's Cathedral choir

The grave of Jonathan Swift

through the hole, thus giving rise to the common expression 'to chance your arm'.

Also in St Patrick's Close (left from the cathedral exit) is **Marsh's Library** 🔟 (Tues, Wed, Thurs & Fri 9.30am–5pm, Sat 10am–5pm; www.marshlibrary.ie). The first public library in Ireland was founded in 1707 and held more than 25,000 books, most dating from the sixteenth to the eighteenth century. The oak shelving is original, as are the metal cages in which scholars were locked so as to prevent thefts. Even if you are not a scholar, do come here – the atmosphere and beauty of the place is entrancing.

GEORGIAN DUBLIN

Georgian architecture is found all over the city; however, the harmonious streets and squares lying to the southeast of Nassau Street truly deserve the title. In addition to superb buildings, there are several important museums and galleries to visit, and the banks of the Grand Canal provide leafy, shaded walks.

MERRION SQUARE

Clare Street, at the eastern end of Nassau Street, runs into **Merrion Square North**, where you will find some of the area's finest houses. The square dates from 1762 – houses here were the homes of high society, including many members of parliament, famous artists, and writers. Look for individual details – the painted doors, the fanlights, and the doorknockers, some in the form of a fish or a human hand.

The **National Gallery of Ireland** 🔟 (Mon 11am–5.30pm, Tuesday, Wed, Thurs, Fri & Sat 9.45am– 5.30pm, Sun 11.30am–5.30pm; www.nationalgallery.ie) houses a fine collection of works from the fourteenth to the twentieth century, from Goya, Brueghel, Titian, Velasquez, Rembrandt, and Gainsborough, to Monet, Degas, and Picasso. One of the gallery's most important paintings – Caravaggio's long-lost masterpiece, *The Taking of Christ* – was discovered in the Jesuit House on Dublin's Leeson Street in 1993. There is also an impressive collection of Irish art, including a whole roomful of Jack Yeats's paintings. There are watercolours,

Georgian doorways on Merrion Square

drawings, prints, sculpture, and a multimedia gallery offering information about a hundred of the gallery's best works. There is a good bookshop and the spacious Winter Garden café.

Guided tours of the Government Buildings (Sat 10.30am–1.30pm) on Merrion Street are available. Tours run every hour on the half hour and take about forty minutes. Free tickets can be collected on the day from the National Gallery of Ireland from 10:00am. The complex houses the offices and meeting rooms of the Taoiseach (Prime Minister) and his cabinet. It was refurbished in the 1990s and the interior rooms of the buildings are a fascinating and tasteful combination of old and new. A magnificent Evie Hone stained-glass window adorns the landing in the main entrance; it is beautifully complemented by the carpet and balustrade designed by Mary Fitzgerald. There is some excellent contemporary furniture

Government buildings

and a miniature of Oisín Kelly's sculpture The Children of Lir. Outside, the courtyard is paved in limestone tram-setts from the streets of Old Dublin.

Next to the front garden of Leinster House, is the **Natural History Museum** (Tues, Wed, Thurs, Fri & Sat 10am–5pm, Sun–Mon 1pm–5pm; www.museum.ie). This museum opened in 1857 with a speech by Dr Livingstone. Set in a compact neoclassical building, it is a wonderful shrine to the late-Victorian obsession with travelling and collecting. Old and young warm to the displays of stuffed animals and birds in glass cases, with Irish fauna on the ground floor and more exotic creatures including an Indian elephant upstairs. Marvel at the huge antlers of the giant Irish deer who roamed Ireland 10,500 years ago, and whose skeletons were preserved in bogs.

Enter one of the many gates of **Merrion Square Park** and walk along some of the secret, wooded paths to the immaculately groomed gardens. Do not miss Danny Osborne's **statue of Oscar Wilde**, wearing a smoking jacket with red lapels and reclining on a rock in the northeast corner of the park. At the height of the Great Famine (1845–1849), a soup kitchen was set up here to feed the starving. You will want to return here to browse the **Boulevard Galleries** of art set up around the square on summer weekends.

FITZWILLIAM SQUARE AND BEYOND

Take the time to stroll down the streets around Merrion Square, which were laid out at the same time. At the eastern end of Mount Street Upper, you will notice the distinctive shape of the Greek-revival **St Stephen's Church**, which dates back to 1824. For obvious reasons it is known universally as the 'Pepper Canister Church'. Occasional events and concerts are held here.

Lower Fitzwilliam Street, at the southeast corner of Merrion Square, houses the offices of the Electricity Supply Board. They

Picture this...

The star exhibits of the Natural History Museum, a species once known as Irish Elk, megaloceros giganteous, has been renamed Giant Deer. They are neither elk, nor exclusively Irish. Standing over 2m- (62.5ft-) tall, with antlers measuring nearly 4m- (13ft-) across, they flourished across Europe during the last Ice Age some 10,500 years ago. In Ireland the skeletons were preserved in bogs following a rise in sea level, and disinterred in the nineteenth century.

tried to make up for the ugliness of their new premises by restoring **Number Twenty Nine** ⑰ (Tue, Wed, Thurs, Fri & Sat 10am–5pm, Sun noon–5pm; www.esb.ie/numbertwentynine) as a museum representing a typical bourgeois house of the period. Indeed, this lovely Georgian townhouse has been superbly fitted out to reflect middle-class life in the late-eighteenth and early–nineteenth century. An audio-visual display, cosily narrated by the 'ghost' of the former owner and her much put-upon maidservant, is followed by a half-hour guided tour for up to ten people. The staff is friendly and helpful, and there is a small tearoom. Try to get there at off-peak times as the place can get very busy.

The street crosses Lower Baggot Street and leads on to **Fitzwilliam Square**, which has a park open to residents only. The last Georgian square built in Dublin, it was laid out in 1792 and the centre was enclosed in 1813. Here, as elsewhere in Georgian Dublin, there is exquisite detail in the doorways, fanlights, and the ironwork of the balconies.

Return to Baggot Street, and turn left (SE) to the junction with Herbert Place. Beyond Baggot Street Bridge to the east is the suburb of **Ballsbridge**, at the heart of which are the grounds of the

Royal Dublin Society (RDS; www.rds.ie) where the famous Dublin Horse Show takes place.

If you turn right at Baggot Street Bridge along the towpath of the **Grand Canal**, you can see a bronze statue of the Irish poet Patrick Kavanagh, who died in 1967; the poet is shown in relaxed pose, on a bench. The pleasant towpath walk, under a canopy of leaves, goes past the gardens of terraced houses, offices, and apartment buildings. There are plenty of ducks, moorhens, and swans, and the canal is spanned by the distinctive curves of the eighteenth-century bridges.

For a total contrast, walk along Herbert Place in the opposite direction and follow the canal to Grand Canal Square, the heart of Dublin's ambitious Docklands Development (www.dublin-docklands.ie) – where plans for public recreations areas include the building of a 'Chocolate Park' – and the location of Daniel Libeskind's stunning theatre. In fine weather kayakers ply the water on Grand Canal Dock, while office workers relax over an outdoor coffee from one of the many food outlets. The headquarters of both Google and Facebook are based in this lively new quarter. From here you can cross to the northside of the Liffey on the beautiful Samuel Beckett Bridge, designed by Santiago Calatrava.

Statue of Oscar Wilde

NORTH OF THE RIVER

Dublin north of the Liffey has its own atmosphere and, like the southern part of the city, some magnificent buildings, museums, and Dublin's two most important theatres.

ALONG THE QUAYS

Crossing **O'Connell Bridge**, there are fine views along the river. The Custom House is on the right and to the left is the equally splendid Four Courts. The almost square O'Connell Bridge opened in 1880 – Bindon Blood Stoney's redesign of James Gandon's Carlisle Bridge. To the north of the river a boardwalk leads to Dublin Discovered Boat Tour (tel 01 473 0000; www.dublindiscovered.ie) where you can take a forty-five--minute-long river cruise on an all-weather

Crossing Fitzwilliam Square in style

boat with live historical commentary on some of Dublin's finest buildings.

Turning left along the quays of the north bank towards the Four Courts (about 1.5km/1 mile), you will reach the cast-iron **Ha'penny Bridge**, which connects Merchants' Arch to Liffey Street. The footbridge was built in 1816; its name refers to the toll once levied for crossing. Looking up river, the next bridge is the pedestrian **Millennium Bridge**. On the corner of Liffey Street is a sculpture known locally as 'the hags with the bags'. Two doors down from the bridge are the charming Winding Stair bookshop and restaurant.

Patrick Kavanagh

Patrick Kavanagh was born in 1904 at Mucker, Inniskeen, County Monaghan. His father eked a living from the land and by repairing the shoes that walked upon it. Young Patrick joined in these trades with little success. Local farmers made a joke of his farming skills and called him a fool for pursuing poetry. He moved to Dublin and in 1936 *Tarry Flynn*, his first publication, set his reputation on its way.

The **Four Courts** (www.courts.ie/four-courts) was built between 1776 and 1802 and designed by Thomas Cooley and James Gandon. The building is a majestic sight with its Corinthian portico crowned with statues, and its columned dome. It holds the various courts of the city. The building was damaged in the fighting of the 1920s, and a fire destroyed all the official archives, but thorough restoration work was carried out in 1932. You can step inside when the courts are in session but check in advance.

Turn north into Church Street to find **St Michan's Church** ❶⑧ (Mar–Oct Mon, Tues, Wed, Thurs & Fri 10am–12.45pm and 2–4.30pm, Sat 10am–1pm; Nov–Mar Mon, Tues, Wed, Thurs & Fri 12.30–3.30pm, Sat 10am–1pm; charge for tours; tel: 01 872

4154). Built in the seventeenth century on the site of a Danish chapel, the church's chief claim to fame is its vaults. Thanks to their limestone composition, the vaults preserve bodies buried there in a mummified state. A few of the bodies are on display. Robert Emmet is thought to be buried in the graveyard of the church, and Parnell's funeral service was held here. Handel is said to have practised on the 1724 organ while composing *The Messiah*.

The **Old Jameson Distillery** ⑲ (daily 9am–6pm, last tour 5.15pm; www.jamesonwhiskey.com;) is in Smithfield, the heart of Old Dublin. If you ever wanted to know more about the fascinating craft of whiskey making, this award-winning attraction is the place to find out. Located on the original site of the Jameson Distillery in cobbled Bow Street, it also offers a history of the distillery itself.

The imposing Four Courts

Behind the building is Smithfield Market, Dublin's fruit, vegetable, and flower market. A traditional horse fair is held here on the first Sunday of March and September, the last vestige of a long tradition of inner-city horse dealing.

If you turn right instead of left from O'Connell Bridge, you will come to one of Dublin's great architectural masterpieces, the **Custom House** **㉒** Designed by James Gandon – his first Dublin masterpiece – it was completed in 1791. The sculpture on the dome (a personification of Commerce) and the river gods (including Anna Livia, set over the main door) are by Edward Smyth, who was also responsible for the statues on the General Post Office. (see page 62). The north side of the building has statues by Joseph Banks depicting Africa, America, Asia and Europe. The Custom House Visitor Centre (daily 10am–4.45pm; https://heritageireland. ie) gives the history of the building, burning and restoration of the Custom House.

On Custom House Quay is Dublin's **Famine Memorial**. Unveiled in 1998, this is a series of striking life-size bronze figures by sculptor Rowan Gillespie. Their gaunt and emaciated features are given added poignancy by the fact that they appear to be walking past the gleaming facade of the Allied Irish Bank, looking east towards the Irish Sea.

O'CONNELL STREET

O'Connell Street is a grand boulevard with a wide central section, studded with monuments and statues. It runs in a straight line north from O'Connell Bridge, and the best way to view it is to walk down the central island, making excursions to the left and right at the pedestrian crossings.

The road was largely destroyed in the Easter Rising (see page 20), but was restored by the end of the 1920s. At the foot of the bridge is John Foley's **monument to Daniel O'Connell**, surrounded by four victory figures and peppered with bullet holes from 1916. Oisín Kelly's memorial to working-class hero, orator, and socialist **Jim Larkin** is opposite the famous chiming clock of the historic **Clerys building**, one of the world's first purpose-built department stores, it was founded in 1853. Farther up on the right is one of Dublin's legendary hotels, the Gresham, which was built in 1817, seven years before the Shelbourne.

In the centre of O'Connell Street is the **General Post Office (GPO) ㉑** (Mon, Tues, Wed, Thurs, Fri & Sat 8.30am–6pm). Built between 1815 and 1818, it is one of the last great buildings to come out of Dublin's Georgian boom, and is renowned for its imposing Ionic portico (look for the bullet holes) with six fluted columns, and figures sculpted by Edward Smyth. It was here, in 1916, that James Connolly and Padraig Pearse barricaded themselves inside and proclaimed the Irish Republic. The post office was virtually destroyed in the fighting but has since been restored. The Rising is commemorated in the main hall by a beautiful bronze statue of the mythic folk hero **Cúchulainn** and by ten paintings illustrating various scenes of the rebellion. There is also the GPO Museum Witness History (Wed, Thurs, Fri & Sat 10am–5pm; July–Sept Tues, Wed, Thurs, Fri & Sat 10am–5pm; www.gpowitnesshistory.ie); an interactive visitor centre

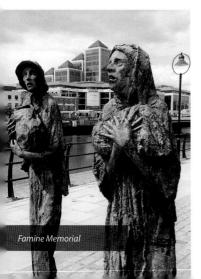

Famine Memorial

which documents the 1916 Easter Rising and modern Irish history.

O'Connell Street has benefited from a renovation programme that created a pedestrian plaza with trees, street furniture, and special lighting in front of the GPO. The **Spire of Dublin** ㉒ was erected in 2003 on the old site of Nelson's Pillar (destroyed by republicans in 1966). It stands 120m- (394ft-) high and a time capsule has been sealed beneath it. From the very start it has been popular among Dubliners as a shiny new monument for their much loved but much battered city. Just off Lower O'Connell Street, and on the corner of Lower Abbey and Marlborough streets is the **Abbey Theatre** (see page 93; www.abbeytheatre.ie). Founded in 1904 by W.B. Yeats, Lady Augusta Gregory and Edward Martyn, the theatre has long been a showcase for great Irish writing. The early works of Sean O'Casey and John Synge were written for the Abbey. The present theatre dates from 1966, since a fire in 1951 destroyed the original. It now forms part of the National Theatre, along with the Peacock Theatre, its smaller scale stage.

Situated just north of the Abbey Theatre in Marlborough Street is **St Mary's Pro-Cathedral** (www.procathedral.ie) the main Catholic parish church of the city centre, built between 1816 and 1825. It has a somewhat forbidding classical Doric exterior and seems to dwarf the street; it was originally designed for O'Connell Street. The domed Renaissance interior is very plain, but the Palestrina choir that sings Mass here on Sundays is anything but, and attracts large numbers of visitors.

Joyce statue

At the junction of O'Connell Street and North Earl Street is a statue of James Joyce, walking with a cane in his hand. Ever-irreverent Dubliners know it as the 'Prick with the Stick'.

Moore Street Market

It is worth making a detour on the pedestrianised areas of **Henry Street** and **Moore Street**, to see their famous markets and hear the cries of the stallholders. Expect some ribald remarks in broad Dublin accents. Moore Street Market is open Monday to Saturday and specialises in fruit, vegetable and flowers. This area is quickly becoming the multiethnic hub of Dublin's growing immigrant community. Alongside the fruit stalls are shops and restaurants selling Russian, African, and Chinese specialities.

At the northern end of the street is the 1911 **monument to Parnell** by Augustus St-Gaudens. Notice anything odd? Yes, he is wearing two overcoats. Apparently, he always did.

PARNELL SQUARE

Compared to the Georgian squares south of the Liffey, the area around **Parnell Square** looks rather shabby, but once it was just as fashionable and affluent. On the south side of Parnell Square are the **Rotunda Hospital** and the Gate Theatre. Between 1751 and 1757, Richard Castle built the Palladian-style Rotunda, Europe's oldest maternity hospital. The chapel on the first floor, with stained-glass windows and Rococo plasterwork, has served at different times as an Assembly Room and a cinema; Charles Dickens also gave readings here. What is now the **Gate Theatre ㉓** (www.

gatetheatre.ie) was built in 1784 and is probably the most beautiful stage in Dublin. The theatre company was founded in 1930 by Michael MacLiammóir and Hilton Edwards, and is still going strong today, with an excellent reputation for international and innovative work. James Mason and Orson Welles began their acting careers here. The theatre is now a popular venue for contemporary music concerts.

The **Garden of Remembrance** on the north side of Parnell Square is dedicated to those who lost their lives in the cause of Irish freedom and features a cruciform lake and Oisín Kelly's beautiful sculpture of the *Children of Lir*.

Across the road from the garden, the **Dublin City Gallery**, **The Hugh Lane** ㉔ (Tues, Wes & Thurs 9.45am–6pm, Fri 9.45am–5pm, Sat 10am–5pm, Sun 11am–5pm; www.hughlane.ie) occupies a home built for Lord Charlemont by Sir William Chambers. This handsome building is worth seeing for itself alone, as well as for the splendid art collection. Sir Hugh Lane, who died in 1915, bequeathed his art collection to the Irish government and the National Gallery in London. The collection includes works by Manet, Degas, and other French impressionists as well as their Irish counterparts. The Post-Impressionist paintings of Jack B. Yeats (brother of the famous poet) are particularly noteworthy. The gallery has also acquired the Studio of Francis Bacon and all its contents, which has been reconstructed here as a permanent exhibit.

Next door, the **Dublin Writers Museum** ㉕ (Mon, Tues, Wed, Thurs, Fri & Sat 9.45am–4.45pm, Sun 11am–4.30pm; June–Aug Mon, Tues, Wed, Thurs & Fri 10am–6pm; tel: 01 872 2077) is an intriguing combination of Georgian exterior and Victorian interior. No one interested in Irish writing and theatre should miss this light and elegant museum covering the long Irish literary tradition, displaying first editions, theatre programmes, correspondence, clothing and other memorabilia, as befits a UNESCO City of Literature. The collection begins with medieval Irish writing and ends with Brendan Behan, Liam O'Flaherty, and Sean O'Faoláin. There are frequent exhibitions and events, and the Writers Centre provides a place for talk and work. Upstairs is a portrait gallery. There is also a children's room, a bookshop, and a good café.

Walk southwest on Parnell Square North and turn right on to Granby Row, then left on to Dorset Street Upper, and right on to Henrietta Street. 14 Henrietta Street (Wed, Thurs, Fri, Sat & Sun 10am–4pm; https://14henriettastreet.ie) was built in the 1740s by Luke Gardiner, and was once one of the finest early Georgian buildings in Dublin. 14 Henrietta Street is a unique social history museum; the story of the house and its inhabitants encapsulates

The Hungry Tree

the history of Dublin – from Georgian heyday to tenement. House tours run every hour from 10am and walking tours at 11.30 am and 2pm. Then head to the bottom of the cul de sac and walk through to Kings Inn Park. Follow the path to your left to see one of the city's natural curiosities, The Hungry Tree.

East of Parnell Square, along North Great George's Street, is the **James Joyce Centre** ㉖ (Oct–March Tues, Wed, Thurs, Fri & Sat 10am–5pm, Sun noon–5pm; April–Sept Mon, Tues, Wed, Thurs, Fri & Sat 10am–5pm, Sun noon–5pm; https://jamesjoyce.ie). This interesting museum and cultural centre are housed in a mansion dating from 1784. The centre contains a library, exhibition rooms, and a study centre devoted to the great novelist. There is a full programme of events, including lectures, tours of the house, and a walking tour of Joycean Dublin. Joyce himself must have known the house as the residence of Mr Denis J Maginni 'professor of dancing', who appears several times in the novel *Ulysses*.

PHOENIX PARK

On the banks of the Liffey, just 3km (2 miles) from the bustle of O'Connell Street, lies **Phoenix Park (daily 7am–10.45pm)** ㉗. Comprising some 709 hectares (1,750 acres) of landscaped gardens, woods, pastures, and playing fields, it is one of the biggest urban parks in Europe, a graceful and elegant expanse with fine views of the mountains, much loved by Dubliners since it was first opened to the public in 1747. Black plaques mark self-guided heritage walks and nature trails, while bikes can be hired at the gate lodge.

The oldest building in the park is **Ashtown Castle**, a former papal residence that has been renovated to house the splendid **Phoenix Park Visitor Centre** (daily 9.30am–6pm; www.phoenixpark.ie), which presents a video and an excellent two-floor exhibition on the history and wildlife of the park. The castle itself comprises an early seventeenth-century tower house, restored with Irish oak from the park, which is held together without a single nail. Outside there is a young garden maze, marking the outline of the original foundations, and a restful café.

The park also has the tallest obelisk in Europe in the 67m-(220ft-) high **Wellington Monument**, erected in 1861 to commemorate Wellington's victory at the Battle of Waterloo. The Wicklow granite is faced with plaques cast from captured and melted-down cannon. Not quite as large is the **Papal Cross**, commemorating Pope John Paul II's visit in 1979, when more than one million people gathered to celebrate Mass.

JAMES JOYCE'S DUBLIN

The Irish Catholic novelist, poet and short story-writer James Joyce (1882–1941) is best known for his controversial novel *Ulysses* (1922), which describes in minute detail a day in the life of advertising salesman Leopold Bloom as he makes his way through the city. Dublin had also played a part in two of Joyce's previous works, the short story collection *Dubliners* (1914), and the semi-autobiographical novel *A Portrait of the Artist as a Young Man* (1914–15). Joyce's descriptions of Dublin life in *Dubliners* are as evocative as they are gloomy – his city is one of 'dark muddy lanes' and 'dark dripping gardens'. Stephen Dedalus, the dissolute protagonist of *A Portrait of the Artist*, views Dublin in similarly despairing tones. This contrasts with Joyce's buoyant characterisation of Dublin in *Ulysses*, which is so rich in detail the author claimed the city could be rebuilt from his book. However, the novel's linguistic complexities and lengthy streams of consciousness discourage many readers.

The **Phoenix Column** (1747) stands near the natural spring that gives the park its name. This was the result of an English corruption of the Gaelic *fionn uisce*, meaning 'clear water'.

The Wellington Monument

Occupying more than 26 hectares (66 acres), **Dublin Zoo** ㉘ (daily 9.30am–3pm; www.dublinzoo.ie) was founded in 1831. The landscaped grounds provide a safe home for more than seven hundred species, including such endangered animals as snow leopards and golden lion tamarinds. Decimus Burton, who was also responsible for the park lodges, designed the grounds. A highlight is the African Plains, which provides a spacious home for large species. The Nakuru Safari tour takes visitors through this area.

Also within the sprawling grounds of the park is the official residence of the Irish president **Áras an Uachtaráin**, (Jan–Dec Sat 10am, 11.15am, 12.30pm, 1.45pm & 3pm; guided tours only; https://president.ie) which dates from 1751, and the US ambassador's residence, the house was formerly the official residence of the Viceroy's chief secretary (not open to the public).

Just to the northwest of Phoenix Park is **Farmleigh House and Estate** (daily 10am–5pm; www.farmleigh.ie). This grand estate of 32 hectares (78 acres) was bought by the government from the Guinness family and has been carefully refurbished. Today the estate is used to accommodate visiting dignitaries, high-level meetings, and for public enjoyment. The interior is beautifully presented and the Victorian Courtyard hosts food markets in the spring and summer.

EXCURSIONS

SOUTH OF THE CITY

As if the city itself did not provide enough options, the countryside around Dublin offers a wealth of possible excursions and day trips. The DART railway, runs north and south along the scenic coast to nearby seaside towns and villages. Whether you take the DART north or south, you will find good sandy beaches.

Dún Laoghaire was once the major port on the east coast, with ferries crossing the Irish Sea to and from Holyhead, but since 2015 the service runs in and out of the Port of Dublin, leaving the harbour free for yachts. West of the harbour is the ramshackle National Maritime Museum of Ireland (daily 11am–5pm; www.mariner.ie). The penultimate stop on the DART is **Bray**

GETTING OUT

Bus tours will take you to the various destinations (see page 122), and some are accessible by city bus. Visit Dublin (www.visitdublin.com) at Suffolk Street has all the information, and can arrange tours. Car hire is available at the same site (see page 118). It is worth hiring a car so you can go at your own pace. The suggestions for excursions in this section can all be done in a day or a half-day from the city. Note that some attractions can only by seen by guided tour, and the last admission to these may be thirty to forty-five minutes earlier than the official closing time.

Inside the Joyce Museum

29, a faded seaside resort with a beach and amusement arcades in County Wicklow. There are splendid views from Bray Head of the harbour and the mountains. You can take the DART on to its terminus at **Greystones**, a pretty coastal town, or you can walk there along the coast from Bray, though parts of the path are in poor condition.

County Wicklow, also to the south of Dublin, rightly deserves its title 'Garden of Ireland' with some of the most spectacular scenery in the country: rugged mountains, steep, wooded river valleys, and deep lakes, as well as charming villages and some notable mansions and gardens.

James Joyce Museum

At Sandycove in County Dublin the **James Joyce Museum** **30** (daily 10am–4pm; Summer daily 10am–6pm in summer; www.james-joycetower.com) is one of the most unusual small museums in

St Kevin

St Kevin, the founder of the monastery at Glendalough, was famed for his patience. One story tells how a bird laid an egg in the palm of his hand. To avoid causing harm, the holy man stayed still until the egg hatched.

or around Dublin. It is housed in a Martello Tower; a series of such towers, some 12m- (40ft-) high and 2.5m- (8ft-) thick, which were constructed along the coast at the beginning of the nineteenth century to guard against invasion by Napoleon. Joyce stayed in the tower only briefly, and it is the setting for the first chapter of Ulysses. Full of Joycean memorabilia including his guitar, waistcoat, correspondence, and rare editions of books and manuscripts, it is a shrine for Joyce enthusiasts. You can take the DART to Glasthule.

Avoca

The picturesque village of **Avoca** ㉛ in County Wicklow became famous as the setting for the BBC TV series *Ballykissangel*. A company of handweavers has been working here since at least 1723, and visitors are able to watch them as they work. Unfortunately, their products are somewhat less distinctive since the place became a popular tourist attraction. There is a colourful shop and a popular café in the small complex of traditional buildings (summer daily 9am–6pm; winter daily 9.30am–5.30pm).

Glendalough

Set in a beautiful landscape, with clear lakes and streams surrounded by steep wooded hills, the sacred site of **Glendalough** ㉜ (www.glendalough.ie) – named from the Irish for 'Valley of the Two Lakes' or Gleann Dá Locha – is in the Wicklow Mountains. It is highly evocative and should not be missed. It was the place chosen by St Kevin for a monastery that over the centuries, became a great spiritual centre of learning, attracting pilgrims from all over Europe. Despite Viking raids, a great fire at the end of the fourteenth century and long years of neglect, many of the original buildings still stand at Glendalough: the eleventh-century round tower – 30m- (100ft-) high and 15m- (50ft-) around the base; a ninth-century barrel-vaulted church known as 'St Kevin's Kitchen'; and the roofless cathedral. There are also scores of Celtic crosses here.

The site can be visited by car, bus tour or by taking St Kevin's bus (www.glendaloughbus.com; depart 11.30am, arrive 12.50pm, return 4.30pm) from the north side of St Stephen's Green, opposite the Mansion House on Dawson Street. The visitor centre (mid-Mar–mid-Oct, daily 9.30am–7pm, mid-Oct–mid-Mar until 5pm; www.glendalough.ie) provides a twenty-minute audio-visual presentation on the history of Irish monasticism, and an exhibition on the geology and wildlife of the area, plus guided tours, but you can wander about on your own. Glendalough's three nature trails take under an hour at a relaxed pace. Glendalough is part of the **Wicklow Mountains National Park** ③③ (www.wicklowmountainsnationalpark.ie), an area of about 200sq km (78sq miles), which includes most of upland Wicklow, with spectacular scenery, wildlife, and rare flora. The

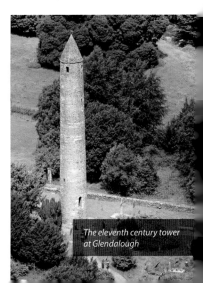

The eleventh century tower at Glendalough

137km- (85-mile) **Wicklow Way** long-distance footpath wends through the park.

Mount Usher Gardens

In 1868, the Walpole family established the spectacular **Mount Usher Gardens** ❸❹ (Ashford, County Wicklow; Mar–Oct daily 10am– 5pm; www.mountushergardens.ie). The climate and soil are such that plants and trees that would not normally survive this far north are capable of flourishing, explaining the enormous variety of more than 4,000 plants, trees, and shrubs from all over the world. It is an 8-hectare (20-acre) paradise, along the River Vartry. It attracts a range of birds and wildfowl. There is also shopping courtyard and an Avoca Garden Café on site.

Powerscourt

About 18km (12 miles) from Dublin, outside the pretty village of Enniskerry in the foothills of the Wicklow Mountains, is **Powerscourt House and Gardens** ❸❺ (Dec–Jan 9.30am–4.30pm; Feb 9.30am–5pm; Mar–Oct 9.30am–5.30pm; Nov 9.30am–4.30pm; www.powerscourt. ie). The gardens are among the greatest in Europe, and take in a view of the Sugar Loaf Mountain as part of their design. Powerscourt consists of some 5,500 hectares (14,000 acres), hugging the River Dargle. This enormous Palladian house was destroyed by fire in 1974. It now incorporates the restored ballroom, a restaurant overlooking the gardens, an exhibition on the history of the estate, several shops, and a garden centre.

The formal splendour of the grounds testifies to the eighteenth-century desire to tame nature, but it is done with such superlative results that one can only be thankful that the work was undertaken. The sweeping terraces offer magnificent views; statuary rears up out of ornamental lakes; deer roam the parklands; and the Dargle obligingly throws itself over 122m (400ft) of rock to form the highest waterfall in Ireland – 4km (2.5 miles) from the main estate. Children also like the pets' cemetery.

Russborough House

Russborough House 36 (Blessington, County Wicklow; house daily 11am–4pm; park daily 9am–6pm; www.russborough.ie) is one of the earliest Irish great houses. A magnificent Palladian mansion, it was designed by Richard Castle and constructed on a monumental scale between 1741 and 1748. A 213m (700ft) facade of Wicklow granite, Doric arcades, and wonderful ornamentation are all set against an impressive terraced landscape, with the extensive grounds covering some 80 hectares (200 acres).

Irish country houses are generally distinguished by their architecture rather than their contents, but Russborough is a striking exception to this rule. The interiors feature superb plasterwork by the Lafranchini brothers, identifiable, as elsewhere, by their trademark of eagles' heads. The plasterwork on the staircase is extraordinary, with its lavish swags of flowers gently held in the mouths of some very patient-looking dogs. The inlaid floors are particularly lovely, and there are extensive collections of furniture, silver, and tapestries.

Also, in the house is the impressive **Beit Collection** of paintings, which is shared with the National Gallery; it

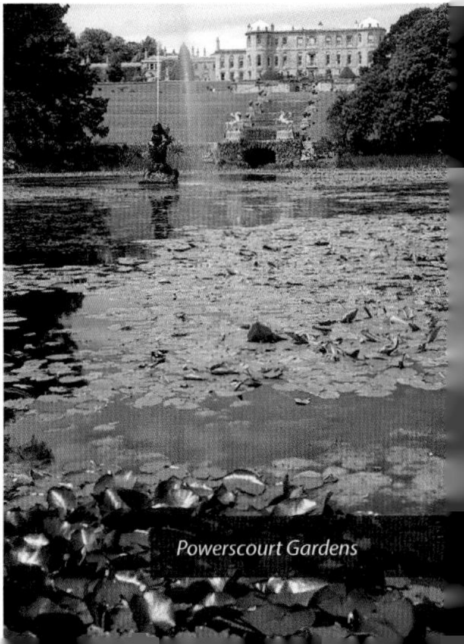

Powerscourt Gardens

includes celebrated works by Gainsborough, Goya, Guardi, Hals, Reynolds, Rubens, Velasquez, Vermeer, and others, plus a series of eight paintings by Murillo depicting the story of the prodigal son.

WEST OF THE CITY

Castletown House ❸ (Cellbridge, County Kildare; Wed, Thurs, Fri, Sat & Sun 10am–12.45pm & 2.15–5pm; tel: 01 16288252; www. castletownhouse.ie) was built between 1722 and 1779 for William Connolly, speaker of the Irish House of Commons. The Palladian facade was designed by Italian architect Alessandro Galilei, and the colonnades and side pavilions by Sir Edward Love Pearce. The result is one of the most graceful and distinctive houses of the period in Ireland. The house's famous Long Gallery has Pompeii fresco-inspired designs and Venetian chandeliers; the great

The trawler dock at Howth

staircase is the work of Simon Vierpyl; and the plasterwork is by the Lafranchini brothers. A 48m- (140ft-) high obelisk adorns the grounds, which are now sadly encroached upon. In addition to the house you can also visit the Biodiversity Garden (daily 10.00am–5pm) and parklands (daily 7am–9pm)

Irish National Stud and Japanese Gardens

Horses are immensely popular in Ireland, and County Kildare can claim to be at the heart of horse country. The Curragh and Punchestown racecourses are situated here, and the **Irish National Stud** ❸ (Feb–Oct daily 10am–6pm; Nov–Dec 10am–4pm; www. irishnationalstud.ie) at Tully. Home to breeding stallions, the national stud has produced some of the most successful horses in the country. Visitors can see horses being trained and exercised. There is also a museum illustrating the history of the horse in Ireland, which features the skeleton of the racehorse Arkle.

Adjacent to the stud are the **Japanese Gardens**, created by the stud's founder in the early part of the century, and well worth a visit, and the **St Fiachras Garden**, created to celebrate the millennium. A combined ticket covers Irish Stud, Irish Horse Museum, Japanese Gardens and St Fiachras Garden.

NORTH OF THE CITY

To the north of Dublin, the DART will take you to the **Howth Peninsula** ❸ (www.visithowth.ie), which affords splendid views along a cliff-top coastal walk above the pretty fishing village. In early summer nesting sea birds abound, as well as interesting land birds and butterflies attracted by the moorland terrain of the cliff top. In July and August there is a wonderful colour combination of purple heather and yellow gorse. When walking up to the lighthouse, it is difficult to believe that Dublin is just a few miles away – until you see Dublin Bay spread out before you. Also located in Howth is the

National Transport Museum (Sat, Sun & Bank Holidays 2–5pm; www.nationaltransportmuseum.org) at Howth Castle.

National Botanic Gardens

Originally modelled on London's Kew Gardens, Ireland's premier horticultural attraction is the **National Botanic Gardens** �40 (summer Mon, Tues, Wed, Thurs & Fri 10am–5pm; Sat & Sun 10am–6pm; winter daily 10am–4.30; www.botanicgardens.ie) at Glasnevin. A short bus ride (No.4 or No.9) north of O'Connell Street, it was established by the Royal Dublin Society in 1795. With over 20,000 species in more than 20 hectares (50 acres) of grounds, there is plenty to see and enjoy in any season. Built between 1843 and 1868, the four magnificently restored glasshouse groups include an alpine house, a palm, and orchid house, and the Curvilinear Range, a spectacular curving glass-house of cast iron.

Nearby is the **Glasnevin Cemetery Museum** (Mon, Tues, Wed, Thurs & Fri 10am–5pm; Sat & Sun 11am–5pm; tours daily 11am & 2pm; www.glasnevinmuseum.ie) – a striking new visitor centre, introducing Dublin's main cemetery, where some of the most notable figures in recent Irish history are buried. These include Charles Stewart Parnell, Daniel O'Connell, and Éamon de Valera.

Casino Marino

The **Casino Marino** �41, (mid-March–May 10.00am–5pm; June–Sept 10am–6pm; Oct 10am–5pm), Lord Charlemont's 'small house by the sea', is regarded as the finest neoclassical building in Ireland. Located on the Malahide Road, 3 miles (5km) from the centre of Dublin, the pleasure house was built between 1755 and 1777, and is indisputably one of William Chambers masterworks. From the outside it looks like a small Greek-style temple, but in fact contains sixteen rooms. To preserve the harmonious design, the four corner columns are hollow to carry water off the roof, and the urns on the roof are disguised chimneys. The interior has exquisite floors and plasterwork. It stands in perfect splendour on a gentle rise. Down the road is 'Spite Crescent', built by an enemy of Lord Charlemont to spoil his view from the Casino. It was here that Bram Stoker stayed while writing *Dracula* (1897).

Malahide Castle

The crenellated **Malahide Castle and Gardens** ❷ (daily 9.30am–5.30pm; www.malahidecastleandgardens.ie) is set in the pretty seaside town of Malahide. Home to the Talbot family for eight hundred years, parts of the building date to the twelfth century. The castle, now publicly owned, contains fine eighteenth-century furniture and displays on the family's history. 9 hectares (22 acres) of ornamental gardens – planted by the Talbot family – contain over 5,000 species. There is also a playground, pitch and putt, and an Avoca café.

Newbridge House and Traditional Farm

Newbridge House ❸ (Apr–Sept daily 9am–5pm; Oct–Mar Tue, Wed, Thurs, Fri, Sat & Sun 10am–4pm; www.newbridgehouseandfarm.com) and its estate of some 142 hectares (350 acres) at Donabate, County Dublin, belonged to the Cobbe family from 1736. The beautifully restored house contains some interesting

Malahide Castle

Winter lottery

The overwhelming demand to see Newgrange during the winter solstice has forced Irish Heritage to hold a lottery. Visitors can sign up in the welcome centre. Or you can email your postal address and contact phone number to brunaboinne@opw.ie and they'll enter your name. From an average 35,000 entries, fifty names are chosen.

furniture and plasterwork, and there is also a courtyard incorporating several artisans' cottages with period furniture and tools, a forge, stables, and a working farm with cows, draught horses, ponies, donkeys, goats, hens, and ducks.

Newgrange

Newgrange ⓮ is the most important of the prehistoric sites around Dublin, located about 3km (2 miles) east of Slane in County Meath. Access is solely by tour from the **Brú na Bóinne Visitor Centre** (Nov–Jan 9.30am–5pm; Feb–Apr & 9.30am–5.30pm, May 9am–6.30pm; June–mid-Sept 9am–7pm; end-Sept 9am–6.30pm; Oct 9.30am–5.30pm; https://heritageireland.ie). Newgrange is the best-preserved passage tomb in Europe. Built around 3200 BC – it predates the earliest Egyptian pyramids, and Stonehenge – and may be the world's oldest solar observatory. The whole edifice is aligned in such a way that for several days during the winter solstice, light from the sun floods the inner chamber for around seventeen minutes, causing a spectacular effect. The guide on the tour attempts to give an idea of this effect by plunging the chamber into darkness and slowly bringing up the light. The sites are busy in summer, and entry cannot be guaranteed. Go early in the day, and allow at least three hours.

Nearby is **Knowth** ⓯ (https://heritageireland.ie), accessible via the Brú na Bóinne Visitor Centre, an even larger and older complex, which dates back to the early Neolithic and has two passage graves.

Tara

Tara 46 is a familiar name in Irish myths and legends. The seat of the high king of Ireland, Tara was the cultural, political, and religious centre of early Irish civilisation and was of particular importance during the Iron Age (600 BC to 400 AD) . However, its importance waned with the arrival of Christianity, and today there is little to see except the hill, the remains of an Iron-Age fort and some pillar stones. In a nearby nineteenth-century Anglican church you'll find the **visitor centre** (late May–Oct daily 9.30am–6pm); facilities include a giftshop, an audio-visual exhibit, and guided tours. Tours depart from the visitor centre and lead past earthworks and ditches with evocative names such as *Rath na Riogh* (Fort of the Kings) and *Dumha Na nGiall* (Mound of the Hostages), a passage tomb that is over 5000 years old.

The prehistoric mound at Newgrange

The local tipple

THINGS TO DO

Time to settle

When you order a Guinness, the bartender fills the glass three quarters and lets it settle before topping it off. Leave it a moment before you take a drink. It should be a smooth, dark black before you tip it back.

Dublin is rapidly becoming a 24-hour city, so there is plenty to enjoy when you've finished sightseeing. The city's many pubs are the centre of social life, offering conversation and a quiet pint, food, music, and song. There are also lots of late-night clubs and bars. With first-class shops and a profusion of booksellers, galleries, and antiques dealers, you can browse or buy contentedly. If you are feeling active, there are also some excellent opportunities to enjoy sports.

PUBS

As you walk through Dublin's streets it will sometimes seem that there is a pub on every corner. Pubs are Ireland's living rooms – they provide not only drink and food, but atmosphere, enter-tainment, and amusing talk. You may not fall into conversation in Dublin quite as readily as in a country pub, but you will find that Dubliners are welcoming hosts. Most pubs also serve food – they are good places to have lunch – and some have dining rooms. Pubs in the O'Connell Street and Temple Bar area now have security guards on the door, vetting customers to ensure a pleasant expe-rience for all. Pubs open at 11am and close at 12.30am, though many pubs in central Dublin stay open later at weekends.

The oldest pub in Dublin is reputedly the Brazen Head (20 Lower Bridge Street) where, it is claimed, a tavern has stood since the twelfth century. Wolfe Tone and the United Irishmen are rumoured

Irish pubs are the best place to meet locals

to have met here to plan their rebellion. It's cosy and intimate, and a good pint of Guinness is served at the bar. Other authentic old Dublin pubs include Toner's (139 Baggot Street Lower) – recommended for whiskey, Mulligan's (8 Poolbeg Street), Ryan's (28 Parkgate Street) and The Long Hall (51 South Great George's Street), reputedly the city's longest bar.

Whatever you are looking for in a pub, Dublin has it in spades. O'Donoghue's (15 Merrion Row), formerly the haunt of The Dubliners, and The Temple Bar Pub (47–48 Temple Bar) are a good bet for traditional music. Jack Nealon's (165 Capel Street) plays jazz on Sundays; look up to see the two-hundred-year-old gilt ceiling. The traditional Slattery's (129 Capel Street) serves up one of the best full Irish breakfast in Dublin. If you're looking for traditional set-dancing, check out O'Shea's Merchant (12 Lower Bridge Street). The Stag's Head (1 Dame Court) is known for its good food, Victorian-style interior, and stand-up comedy.

Off Grafton Street, Kehoe's (9 South Anne Street) is a favourite watering hole. If you're on a Joycean odyssey drop by Davy Byrne's (21 Duke Street) – where Leopold Bloom ate a gorgonzola sandwich and drank a glass of wine – and The Bailey Bar (1–4 Duke Street), a busy, trendy, and gay-friendly bar on the site of Leopold Bloom's house. In Neary's Bar & Lounge (1 Chatham Street) you will probably encounter a theatrical crowd, it's behind the Gaiety Theatre. For craft beer try The Porterhouse Central (45–47 Nassau Street).

There are many beautiful old pubs in Temple Bar, but they are often choked with tourists. It's best to avoid weekend evenings when exploring haunts such as the Oliver St John Gogarty (58-59 Fleet Street), named for the poet, playwright, and surgeon (and model for a character in Ulysses). The cosy Ha'penny Bridge Inn (42 Wellington Quay) is a good spot for live music and the afore-mentioned The Temple Bar attracts a lively crowd; The Norseman (28 East Essex Street) is a favourite of Dublin's art crowd, while the Auld Dubliner (24–25 Anglesea Street) is a pleasant pub that caters largely to tourists. The Palace Bar (21 Fleet Street) has a beautiful interior and buzzy atmosphere; it's popular with journalists from the nearby *Irish Times*. Doheny & Nesbitt's (5 Baggot Street Lower), with its snugs and mirrored partitions, is famous for political debate. Cabinet ministers, legal eagles, and journalists in search of visiting celebrities favour the Horseshoe Bar at the Shelbourne Hotel (27 St. Stephen's Green). If you are after a taste of modern Dublin, then there are chic, sleek pubs dotted throughout the city. The Market Bar (14 Fade Street) is an enormous bar and tapas restaurant that oozes charm despite its size.

SHOPPING

The main shopping areas are in and around Grafton Street, and north of the river around O'Connell Street and Henry Street.

Shoppers on Grafton Street

Grafton Street is lined with well-known chains, plus the excellent, upmarket Brown Thomas department store. Smaller, hipper boutiques have sprung up in the former rag trade district west of Grafton Street, known as the Creative Quarter. O'Connell Street and pedestrianised Henry Street tend towards more ubiquitous stores, but two landmarks can be found there: Eason's flagship bookstore (40 Lower O'Connell St), and Arnotts department store (12 Henry Street).

SHOPPING CENTRES

St Stephen's Green Shopping Centre (www.stephensgreen. com) is at the top of Grafton Street and overlooks the famous urban park. It has three floors of shops, but none really stand out and many are chains. However, there is a large Dunnes Stores – an Irish clothing and groceries chain – on the ground floor, with good value diffusion lines for Irish designers across fashion and homeware. There is also a large Boots pharmacy and an Eason's bookstore. The small upmarket **Westbury Mall on Balfe Street,** with jewellers, galleries, and craft and design shops is worth a walkthrough, and connects with Clarendon Street. The **Powerscourt Townhouse** (www.powerscourtcentre.ie), the grand dame of the Creative Quarter, houses antique, jewellery, and designer clothing stores. You'll find classic rainwear at Francis Campelli (46

South William Street) and sophisticated minimalism at the Helen McAlinden Boutique (20 South William Street). For vintage clothing and jewellery drop by Jenny Vander (50 Drury Street), and for high-fashion browse Costume (10 Castle Market). Stop by Avoca (11–13 Suffolk Street) for Irish craft and design.

The **Royal Hibernian Way links Grafton Street to Dawson Street.** It underwent a major refurbishment in 2018, and now offers good eateries as well as relaxed shopping in elegant stores. Dawson Street is lined with bookshops and boutiques.

North of the river, the **Jervis Centre** (www.jervis.ie) on Abbey Street Upper has a selection of fashion, leisure, and technology stores. At the **ILAC Centre** (www.ilac.ie) on Henry Street, you will find a range of outlets such as TK Maxx, The Perfume Shop, and Dunnes Stores. Younger travellers should enjoy browsing the family-run Banba Toymaster (48 Mary Street). The Moore Street Mall (www.moorestreetmall.ie) on Parnell Street specialises in ethnic stores from Brazil, Lithuania, Poland and African countries.

MARKETS

Dublin's oldest market is on **Moore Street** (Mon, Tues, Wed, Thurs, Fri & Sat 10am–4pm). This traditional open-air market is famous for the cries of its sellers, on whom the well-known song Molly Malone is modelled. Flowers, fruit, vegetables, electronics and a little bit of everything else are on sale here. It is also the place to go to pick up ethnic food and goods.

Pretty **George's Street Arcade** (Mon, Tues & Wed 9am–6pm, Thurs, Fri & Sat 9am–7pm, Sun noon–6pm) is a covered market between South Great George's and Drury streets. Stores and stalls line this atmospheric little market – a good place for second-hand books, art, music, vintage clothing, and a variety of ethnic ware.

The **Temple Bar Food Market** (Sat 10.30am–4pm) at Meeting House Square is great for speciality foods and gourmet delights.

Temple Bar Food Market

It's also worth heading to the Old City section of Temple Bar where you will find a good range of chic interiors stores and the trendy Cow's Lane Fashion and Design Mart (Sat 10am–5pm) with its innovative designers. Further afield, the popular **Blackrock Market** (19a Main Street, Blackrock; Sat & Sun 11am–5.30pm) hosts over thirty stalls selling jewellery, crafts, books, antiques, and clothes.

WHAT TO BUY

Antiques. Don't miss a stroll down Francis Street. Dublin's 'antiques highway' is lined with antique and art stores. These include Michael Connell Antiques – Victorian and Edwardian furniture, silver, brassware, and china; Martin Fennelly Antiques – decorative art, fine furniture, paintings, and lamps; and Johnston Antiques – fine Irish Georgian furniture. Also check out the lovely antique shops on the second floor of Powerscourt Townhouse and stalls in George's Street Arcade.

Art. For contemporary art, you should try the Kerlin Gallery (Anne's Lane, South Anne Street; www.kerlingallery.com), the Taylor Galleries (16 Kildare Street; www.taylorgalleries.ie), or the Oliver Sears Gallery (33 Fitzwilliam Street Upper; www.oliversearsgallery.com). The Temple Bar Gallery (5–9 Temple Bar; www.templebargallery.com) exhibits the work of contemporary artists, and the Oriel Gallery (17 Clare Street; www.theoriel.

com) has an equally impressive and more accessible collection of original art for sale.

Books. Easons (40 Lower O'Connell Street; www.easons.com) is a huge store with mainstream books, magazines, newspapers, and art supplies. Hodges Figgis (56–58 Dawson Street) – of Ulysses fame – carries an excellent selection of literature, general books, books on Ireland, and the works of Irish writers. International Books (18 South Frederick Street; www.internationalbooks.ie) specialises in languages. For antiquarian books, go to Ulysses Rare Books (10 Duke Street; www.rarebooks.ie). In Temple Bar, visit the Gallery of Photography (Meeting House Square; https://www.photobooks.site) bookshop and the Gutter Bookshop (Cow's Lane; www.gutterbookshop.com) – one of Dublin's finest. Books Upstairs (17 D'Olier Street; www.booksirish.com), has an interesting selection of Irish titles, including poetry. The labyrinthine Winding Stair (40 Lower Ormond Quay; www.winding-stair.com) is an intriguing second-hand bookshop beneath a restaurant.

Chocolates. Delicious Irish handmade chocolates can be bought at Butlers Chocolate Café (51 Grafton Street).

Crafts. The most distinguished place for modern Irish crafts is DESIGNyard (25 South Frederick Street; www.designyard.com) with its outstanding selection of jewellery, sculpture, and contemporary design. The Irish Celtic Craftshop (10–12 Lord Edward Street; www.irishcelticcraftshop.com) offers more traditional crafts. The Kilkenny Shop (6 Nassau Street; www.kilkennyshop.com) is a good hunting ground for everything from John Rocha-designed Waterford Crystal to Orla Kiely designer wellies.

Ireland is well-known for its fine crystal, with famous brands including Waterford Crystal, Cavan, Galway, Tipperary, and Tyrone Crystal. Irish designers have designed contemporary lines for Waterford Crystal (John Rocha) and Tipperary Crystal (Louise Kennedy). Prices do not vary. The larger department stores, such as

Brown Thomas on Grafton Street, are good places to find designer crystal lines.

Family Crests. There are a vast number of shops specialising in coats of arms on everything from plaques to keychains. Try Heraldic Artists (www.heraldicartists.com) and House of Names (www.houseofnames.ie), both on Nassau Street.

Food. The Irish supermarket chain, Dunnes Stores (outlets on Middle Abbey Street, St Stephen's Green Shopping Centre, and the ILAC Centre) sells Irish smoked salmon: ask for the wild, not farmed, variety. For Irish country cheeses, go to Sheridan's Cheesemongers (11 South Anne Street; https://sheridanscheesemongers.com) or Listons (25–26 Lower Camden Street; www.listonsfoodstore.ie).

Knitwear. There are two kinds of knits for sale: expensive traditional handknit sweaters and sweaters 'handknit' (hand-loomed) on a machine. The Kilkenny Shop (6 Nassau Street) carries a large variety of knitwear and handwoven goods. Monaghan's (Royal Hibernian Way) specialises in cashmere for men. Bringing knitting into the twenty-first century is This is Knit (Powerscourt Townhouse Centre; https://thisisknit.ie), which has a fabulous range of wool and patterns.

Linens. Brown Thomas has a great linen department, as does Murphy Sheehy (2 Cranford Centre, Stillorgan Road, Dublin 4).

Music. Spindizzy Records (32 Market Arcade, South Great George's Street; www.spindizzyrecords.com) and Claddagh Records (2 Cecilia Street, Temple Bar; www.claddaghrecords.com) carry a good selection of traditional Irish and other local and international artists and you can't miss Tower Records (7 Dawson Street; www.towerrecords.ie).

Photography. If you're looking for memory cards, batteries, and photo printers, try the Camera Centre (56 Grafton Street; www.camera.ie) or John Gunn Camera Shop (16 Wexford Street; www.johngunn.ie).

Pottery and Porcelain.
Kilkenny Shop (6 Nassau Street) has a fine selection.

Souvenirs. Shopping for souvenirs should be an easy task in Dublin. Nassau Street is the best destination for souvenir shopping on the fly. Some shops may not be too original, but they have all the usual crowd-pleasing trinkets. If you have more time, there are some excellent shops spread throughout the city showcasing Irish crafts and design.

Kitsch souvenirs

Toys. Banba Toymaster (https://banbatoys.ie) on Mary Street. Avoca (www.avoca.com) and Arnotts (www.arnotts.ie) also have extensive toy departments.

Wine. For a tasty alternative to the world of Guinness and whiskey, try Mitchell and Sons (CHQ Building, 54 Glasthule Road, Sandycove).

ENTERTAINMENT

THEATRE

Dublin has a proud tradition in theatre, which is still very much alive, so advance booking is advisable. The **Abbey Theatre** (26–27 Lower Abbey Street) is Ireland's national theatre. Once on the cutting edge, today its more experimental repertoire is presented on its second, basement stage, the intimate **Peacock**. The **Gate**

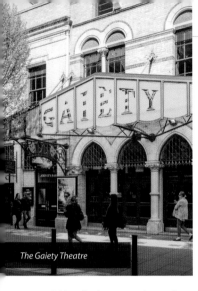
The Gaiety Theatre

Theatre (Cavendish Row, Parnell Square) has a similar tradition, and stages a cosmopolitan mix of Irish and international theatre plus musical acts. It is known for showcasing important new Irish playwrights.

The Victorian **Olympia** (72 Dame Street; www.olympia.ie) is the venue for all sorts of popular theatre, concerts and variety shows. The **Gaiety Theatre** (South King Street; www.gaietytheatre.ie) is worth visiting for its ornate decor alone. It runs a range of productions from plays to variety acts. For innovative theatre, the **Project Arts Centre** (39 East Essex Street; www.projectartscentre.ie) has a lively programme of dance, drama, and performance arts. The **Samuel Beckett Theatre** (www.tcd.ie/beckett-theatre) at Trinity College is mainly for drama students. Theatre productions, opera and ballet, and major international acts feature at the splendid Daniel Libeskind-designed Bord Gáis Energy Theatre (Grand Canal Square; www.bordgaisenergytheatre.ie).

Other theatres of note include the **Civic Theatre** (www.civictheatre.ie) outside the city in Tallaght, with its broad repertoire of music, drama, and comedy productions, and the **3Arena** (Northwall Quay; www.3arena.ie) entertainment venue. The most important event of the theatre season is the **Dublin Theatre Festival** (www.dublintheatrefestival.ie), held in September and October each year. A fringe festival precedes this event.

COMEDY

The International Bar (23 Wicklow Street; www.theinternational-comedyclub.com) has started the careers of many Irish comedians and is still going strong. The revamped Laughter Lounge (8 Eden Quay; www.laughterlounge.com) is Ireland's premier comedy spot with gigs on Thursday, Friday and Saturday nights.

IRELAND'S NATIONAL THEATRE

Dublin's first theatre opened in 1637, and thereafter the city produced many notable playwrights, including Sheridan, Goldsmith, Wilde, and Shaw. However, there was nothing particularly 'Irish' about their work. W. B. Yeats wanted to create a distinctly Irish theatre of poetic drama, and he turned to the legends of ancient Ireland for inspiration. He found a backer in Lady Augusta Gregory, who became his partner. Their first productions were done on a shoestring budget, wherever they could find a space. Finally, in 1904, they acquired a theatre of their own, and the Abbey was born.

The Abbey's career was not without controversy. J. M. Synge's play, The *Playboy of the Western World*, now recognised as a masterpiece, provoked a riot when it was first staged. *The Plough and the Stars*, by the Abbey's first great realist playwright, Sean O'Casey, caused similar public outrage, and the police were called to protect the theatre.

After Yeats' death in 1939, the Abbey entered a period of limbo, although its acting tradition continued to be world renowned. Things turned around with the opening of its new theatre in 1966 and the emergence of new Irish playwrights – Brian Friel, Conor McPherson, and Frank McGuinness among others. Today, the Abbey continues its tradition of commitment to new work by Irish authors in both English and Gaelic.

CLASSICAL MUSIC AND OPERA

The National Symphony Orchestra can be heard in a year-round programme of concerts at the **National Concert Hall** (NCH) (Earlsfort Terrace; www.nch.ie). The NCH also hosts jazz and traditional music evenings. Chamber music concerts and recitals are given at the **Irish Museum of Modern Art** (Royal Hospital Kilmainham; www.imma.ie). **St Anne's Church** (Dawson Street) has lunchtime concerts. Dublin Castle, St Patrick's Cathedral and the Hugh Lane Gallery host occasional concerts. Another venue for classical music is the huge **Helix** (https://thehelix.ie) complex at the Dublin City University campus on Collins Avenue. Dublin also has a number of music festivals (see page 99).

Opera Ireland offers short spring and winter seasons based on the standard repertoire at the **Gaiety Theatre** (www.gaietytheatre.

Concert at Vicar Street

ie) in South King Street. The small but enterprising Opera Theatre Company (www.opera.ie) does two or three performances a year of short operas by contemporary Irish or baroque composers.

ROCK, FOLK AND JAZZ

One of Dublin's largest venues is the **3Arena** (www.3arena.ie) on East Link Bridge, which hosts major pop and rock acts. The RDS (www.rds.ie) in Ballsbridge also occasionally holds huge open-air concerts. *The Irish Times* carries listings for all events in its Friday supplement, *The Ticket*, and the *Evening Herald* has up-to-the-minute information (or see www.entertainment.ie). Some of the best music is heard at the mid-size venues: the **Olympia Theatre** (www.olympia.ie), Vicar Street (www.vicarstreet.com), off Thomas Street, and **the Button Factory (**www.buttonfactory.ie**)** in Temple Bar. **Whelans** (25 Wexford Street; www.whelanslive.com) is a good place to hear up-and-coming artists while the Sugar Club (8 Lesson Street Lower; www.thesugarclub.com) is a stylish spot for live jazz, blues, and Latin music. Jazz and blues fans should also try the upstairs bar at Arthur's (28 Thomas Street; www.arthurspub.ie) in the Liberties.

DANCE

For traditional Irish dancing, go to **O'Shea's Merchant** (12 Lower Bridge Street; www.osheasmerchant.com). **Cultúrlann na hÉireann** (www.comhaltas.ie) holds concerts, stage shows and traditional dances in Monkstown.

FILM

The historical **Savoy Cinema** (16–18 O'Connell Street Upper; www.imccinemas.ie) is the main location for the big new-releases. Art-house and international films are shown at the **Irish Film Institute** (6 Eustace Street; www.ifi.ie). In summer, open-air movies are screened in Meeting House Square in Temple Bar.

NIGHTCLUBS

Nightclubs come and go, so check listings in publications like *The Ticket*, or online.

Leeson Street, always popular for late-night dance clubs, is now dotted with lap-dancing clubs. However, some of the old haunts like Leggs remain. Star-spotters can run the door-policy gauntlet at Krystle (21–25 Harcourt Street; www.krystlenightclub.com), or for a more indie vibe try The Academy (57 Middle Abbey Street; www.theacademydublin.com).

The George (89 South Great George's Street; www.thegeorge.ie) has long been a favourite nightspot for Dublin's LGBTQ community (and visitors).

TRADITIONAL MUSIC

The word *seisiún* – meaning an impromptu evening of music and song, usually in a pub – has a particular resonance for the Irish, and there is plenty of opportunity in Dublin to enjoy traditional Irish sounds. A *seisiún* may start when someone – probably the innocent-looking man sitting in the corner huddled over a pint of Guinness – produces a guitar as if from nowhere, and his neighbour responds by bringing out a well-concealed *bodhrán* (goatskin traditional Irish drum). Soon everyone is joining in.

The mainstay of traditional music is the fiddle. The guitar is something of a latecomer, having arrived around the 1960s, but is now well established. Other instruments you may hear are the *uillean* pipes (softer than the Scottish bagpipe), the six-hole wooden flute, the tin whistle, the accordion, and the banjo, a nineteenth-century transfer from America.

While the real centre of traditional music is in the west, you will find it played in pubs across Dublin; look for listings or signs in the pubs.

SPORTS

GOLF

There are many superb courses in and around Dublin. The Royal Golf Club at Dollymount and many other clubs' welcome visitors. For further information visit www.golfireland.ie; www.visitdublin.com; or www.discoverireland.com/golf.

A night on the town

FISHING

Sea angling is permitted all year, but river fishing requires a licence. Information can be obtained from Dublin's tourist offices or any fishing shop.

SPECTATOR SPORTS

The traditional Irish games of **hurling** and **Gaelic football** are played at Croke Park. **Horse racing** takes place at Leopardstown; at the Curragh (flat racing) and Punchestown (National Hunt racing) in County Kildare. The premiere **show jumping** event is the Dublin Horse Show at the RDS. **Greyhound racing** is on at Shelbourne Park, Ringsend, and at Harold's Cross Stadium. **Rugby** and international **football** (soccer) are played at the Aviva Stadium in Ballsbridge.

WATERSPORTS/BEACHES

The best beaches are in the south, at Bray and Killiney. At Sandycove there's the **Forty Foot** bathing spot, once a men-only nude beach, now open to everyone. It is not advisable to swim within 8km (5 miles) of the city centre because of pollution.

DUBLIN FOR CHILDREN

There are plenty of things for children to enjoy in Dublin. Children under five travel for free on all public transport. Visit https://www.transportforireland.ie/fares/ for further information.

The Ark (11a Eustace Street; www.ark.ie) in Temple Bar is a cultural centre offering a changing programme of plays, workshops, readings, and performances, all geared towards youngsters. It is best to book in advance. **Imaginosity** (Sandycove, Dublin 18; www.imaginosity.ie) is an interactive children's museum for children under the age of nine.

Museums that will appeal to children include the **Natural History Museum** (see page 55) and the **National Wax Museum Plus** (22–25 Westmoreland Street). There are nature trails in **Phoenix Park** and **Dublin Zoo** has a pet corner and zoo train (see page 69).

Older children should enjoy **Dublinia** (see page 45), a lively recreation of medieval Dublin. The self-guided **Rock 'n' Stroll Trail** (www.dublintown.ie/rock-n-stroll-trail) around Dublin, which follows in the footsteps of Irish rock legends, should appeal to the teenage crowd. Also popular are the **Viking Splash Tours** (start point St Stephen's Green; www.vikingsplash.ie), an adventurous tour by land and water in an amphibious vehicle.

For a breath of fresh air, head to **Herbert Park** in Ballsbridge to feed the ducks or to enjoy one of its two playgrounds or relax in **The Giant's Garden** on **Merrion Square** which has climbing frames and swings to entertain. Further out, sprawling **Marlay Park** in Rathfarnham has a miniature railway and a farmer's market on Saturdays.

FESTIVALS AND EVENTS

January *TradFest Temple Bar*, Dublin 2 – lively traditional and folk music festival.

February *Dublin International Film Festival; Rugby Six Nations Championships,* Aviva Stadium, Ballsbridge. *Dublin Racing Festival,* Leopardstown.

March *Dublin International Film Festival; St Patrick's Day Parade.*

April *Handel's Messiah*: commemorative concert held April 13 on Fishamble Street, Temple Bar, the anniversary of its premiere in 1742.

May *International Literature Festival Dublin*: Ireland's premier literary event, attracting the world's finest writers; *International Dance Festival Ireland:* various venues, a range of contemporary dance performances from top international companies; *Dublin Gay Theatre Festival.*

June *Bloomsday*: Dublin city centre and Joyce Museum, Sandycove, a celebration of Joyce and Ulysses; *Dublin Pride; Dublin Kite Festival. Trinity Summer Series* (popular contemporary artists from around the world hold concerts from late June into July).

July *Longitude Festival*: Marlay Park, large-scale contemporary music festival featuring hip-hop artists, indie bands, and singer-songwriters; *Street Performance World Championships*: street performers from all over the world compete in Merrion Square. *Festival of Curiosity* featuring virtual and live events suitable for various age groups around art and design and science and technology.

August *Dublin Horse Show*: RDS, Ballsbridge; *Dublin City Liffey Swim.*

September *All-Ireland Hurling and Football Finals*: Croke Park; *Dublin Fringe Festival*: offbeat sister to the main theatre festival. *Taste of Dublin* foodie-heaven multi-day event.

September/October Dublin Theatre Festival.

October *Dublin City Marathon*: a run through the historic streets. *Bram Stoker Festival.*

November *Dublin Book Festival*

December *National Crafts Fair of Ireland*: RDS, Ballsbridge; *Leopardstown Christmas Racing Festival* – one of the most popular horse racing events of the year; *Winterlights* and *Christmas Markets.*

FOOD AND DRINK

The days of overcooked cabbage, mountains of boiled potatoes, and cholesterol-laden fried meat are long gone in Dublin. Not only is there a new Irish cuisine, created by imaginative young chefs, but ethnic restaurants of all kinds give a wider choice than ever before.

Of course, Dublin has always had the fresh ingredients for a fine cuisine. Situated as it is on the broad sweep of Dublin Bay, with the waters of the Atlantic nearby and a plethora of streams and rivers, the city has access to both sea and freshwater fish in abundance. Here you will find succulent oysters, freshly caught lobster and crab, wild salmon, sole and pike. Tender lamb comes from Kerry and Wicklow; Farmhouse cheese – unique to a particular cheese-maker – is produced throughout the country and has begun to achieve a worldwide reputation. Irish breads, apple tarts, and fruit-cakes have always been delicious, as has traditional Irish cuisine, though it's prepared now with greater delicacy and lightness of touch, and increasingly with some international flair.

MEALS AND MEAL TIMES

Breakfast is either the 'continental' variety – bread, butter, jam, and fruit, served with coffee or tea – or traditional Irish, which generally means robust portions of fried eggs, bacon, tomatoes, sausages, black-and-white pudding, and toast, washed down with coffee or strong tea. Most hotels and restaurants serve breakfast from around 7am until about 10am.

Lunch is served from around noon until 3pm. Many of the more expensive restaurants offer three or four course set lunches, but you can also find simple salads, sandwiches or hot meals at most pubs, cafés and snack bars. Most cafés serve snacks and light meals all day from 8.30 or 9am until 6pm, though many stay open as late as 2am.

Dinner hours usually begin around 6pm with last service at around 10pm. Many restaurants offer pre-theatre or 'early bird' dinner up to 7.30pm, which is usually a good deal. Fixed-price meals are often the best value.

WHERE TO EAT

The choice in Dublin ranges from elegant restaurants, often with French or modern Irish cuisine, to the humble chip shop offering crispy batter-coated portions of tasty fish and chips (try the famous Leo Burdock's at 2 Werburgh Street, near the castle). In between, there are pubs, bistros, and moderately priced restaurants of all kinds. Dublin's restaurants range from those serving traditional

The elegant Café en Seine, on Dawson Street

dishes to Chinese, Indian, Japanese, Mongolian, Romanian, Thai, vegetarian cuisine and more.

There are also cafés, self-service snack bars, and the usual fast-food places. Standards of service can vary considerably from one place to the next, but most establishments are welcoming and friendly. Pubs and bars are a good choice for lunch. For our selection of places to eat, see page 106.

Cafés and restaurants in museums, great houses and other attractions are often superior to comparable eateries picking up the traffic outside. They offer everything from pastries and snacks to hot meals with wine. A nice spot is the Irish Film Institute, in the Temple Bar district. Another excellent café-restaurant is in the intimate vaulted basement of the Irish Museum of Modern Art, and the National Gallery of Ireland's Gallery Café is a good place for pastries.

Cafés and Tearooms

Dublin's abandonment of tea in favour of coffee is notable on the streets, but traditional high tea is still going strong in the city's grand hotels, such as the Shelbourne, Westbury, and the Gresham. To the background strains of soothing Irish harp or tinkling piano music, a liveried waiter will bring you a pot of freshly brewed tea and a silver tray laden with dainty, delicious-looking sandwiches, scones, sweet cakes, and pastries.

Dublin is full of cafés where you can get an excellent cup of coffee (and tea if you prefer) along with a pastry, or a more substantial meal. Cafés are one of the best places to sit and watch the world rush by. Bewley's Oriental Café on Grafton Street has been a go-to destination since 1927, and the tiny but perfect Queen of Tarts on Cork Hill, Dame Street (also Cows Lane), is aptly named. There are plenty of delicatessens and sandwich bars that cater for the lunch hour trade and many of these are very good indeed.

WHAT TO EAT

Starters and Main Courses

It is no surprise that **fish** and **seafood** figure widely on Dublin menus. Wild Irish salmon tops the list. It can be poached, roasted, or steamed, and is generally served simply with light sauces or just a slice of lemon. Alternatively, smoked salmon is a popular choice and is served thinly sliced as a starter or with scrambled eggs as a brunch dish. Cured organic salmon is a popular starter at Dublin's finer restaurants.

Dublin Bay prawns are also very popular, however you choose to eat them – plump, juicy, and delicious. Galway Bay oysters are scrumptious, pair with a pint of Guinness. A variety of freshwater fish, mussels from Wexford (try the mussel soup), Donegal crab, West Cork King Scallops, and Dingle Bay lobster complete the list.

Meat in Irish restaurants is generally served simply to allow the fine flavour to speak for itself. The lamb in Ireland is of the highest quality and features frequently on city menus in guises such as herb-crusted rack of lamb. Irish beef is also a favourite, prime Irish rib-eye and fillet steak is served with elegant sauces, seasonal vegetables, and fondant potatoes. Venison is another popular choice

A bowl of Irish stew

at quality restaurants, as is rabbit and hare. Pork also features strongly, from roast belly to herb-accented gourmet sausages, served simply with mash.

Vegetarians are particularly well catered for in Dublin. There are quite a few specialist and semi-specialist vegetarian restaurants, and often you will have a choice between dishes like vegetable couscous, or parsnips stuffed with brazil nuts, and vegetables in a red pepper sauce. Wholesome pasta dishes can be found in Dublin's many Italian restaurants; they are usually a good bet for vegetarian options. Vegetarian stalwart, Cornucopia on Wicklow Street serves such a variety of tasty daily specials; you may decide not to eat anywhere else while in the capital.

Bread, Pastries and Desserts

Wonderful freshly baked Irish breads have long been a staple of Dublin cuisine. Unfortunately, the pseudo-croissant is now ubiquitous, but happily so are soda bread, wholemeal bread, and all manner of scrumptious scones. Old-fashioned classic Irish confections like porter cake and barmbrack ('báirín breac' or 'brack', made with sultanas and raisins, and popular around Halloween) can also still be found.

TRADITIONAL FARE

Traditional Irish dishes are now being re-worked for a younger market. Some old-fashioned dishes to look for include colcannon (mashed potatoes with leeks and cabbage), *crubeens* (pigs' trotters), *coddle* (boiled bacon, sausages, onions, and potatoes), *boxty* (a tasty potato pancake filled with meat, vegetables or fish), Dublin Lawyer (lobster, flamed in whiskey and simmered in cream) and, of course, the traditional Irish stew, made with lamb, potatoes, and vegetables.

Whatever your choice of dessert (but especially if you select apple tart), you'll usually be asked if you want cream with it. Dessert cakes, puddings, and ice-cream dessert combinations tend to be sweet and rich, so be prepared for a major test of your dietary resolve.

DRINKS

Dublin would not be Dublin without the world-famous stout: **Guinness**, which really does taste better here

Bewley's Oriental Café

than anywhere else. The pouring and settling process takes a little time, but it is worth the wait. Murphy's and other Irish stouts are also wonderful. Don't miss the range of ales and IPAs now available from microbreweries.

There is also a great array of distinctive Irish **whiskeys** – you will see their names etched in the glass of pub windows. **Wine** is readily available, with a fine selection of Australian cabernets and chardonnays, plus Californian, and Chilean wines. Light Italian reds also feature prominently on wine lists. The cheapest way to order wine is to ask for a carafe of the house wine with your meal. Look out for places that allow diners to BYOB (bring your own bottle, sometimes just BYO), and check the corkage charge. Remember that VAT is charged on wine. It's generally cheaper in Dublin to drink in pubs, rather than hotel bars. Prices are highest in the city centre but in general alcohol is expensive in Ireland, even in supermarkets.

WHERE TO EAT

We have used the following symbols to give an idea of the price for an average meal for one, including a service charge of ten to fifteen percent but excluding wine or other drinks:

€€€€   **over 45 euros**
€€€   **30–45 euros**
€€   **20–30 euros**
€   **below 20 euros**

CITY CENTRE SOUTH

777 €€ *7 Castle House, South Great George's Street; Mon–Wed 5.30–10pm, Thu until 11pm, Fri–Sat until midnight, Sun 2–10pm; tel: 01-425 4052; www.777. ie.* Fun Mexican restaurant with bold flavours and vibrant colours, offering Dublin's largest selection of tequilas. Famous for their Margaritas, and the tapas-style menu with dishes to share.

Bewley's Grafton Street Café € *78–79 Grafton Street, Dublin 2; Mon, Tues, Wed, Thurs & Fri 8.30am–5pm, Sat & Sun 9.30am–6pm; tel: 01 672 7720; www. bewleys.com.* No one should miss a trip to the original Bewley's Oriental Café with its Arts and Crafts stained-glass windows. Delicious fair trade coffee, teas, and a range of dishes are on offer for breakfast, lunch, and dinner. The location is perfect for a quick pit-stop while shopping and it's a popular meeting spot with locals and tourists alike. Visit the Bewley's Theatre (www. bewleyscafetheatre.com) for lunchtime and evening musical and theatrical performances.

Café en Seine € *39–40 Dawson Street, Dublin 2; daily noon–11.30pm; tel: 01 677 4567; www.cafeenseine.ie.* Stunning Art Deco interior with three-storey atrium featuring intimate bars within bars. The casual, contemporary food – dry aged Irish beef, sustainable seafood, freshly baked bread – is on offer all day and well into the night. The menu is rich with something for every taste, all at prices your pocket will love. It's a lovely place to stay on for a drink afterwards too.

La Cave €€ *28 South Anne Street, Dublin 2; Mon, Tues, Wed, Thurs, Fri & Sat 12pm–2am, Sun 5pm–2am; tel: 01 679 4409; www.lacavewinebar.com.* Dublin's oldest authentic French wine bar, atmospherically decorated with nostalgic Gallic posters and prints, pairs reasonably priced, flavoursome bistro-style dishes – the two- and three- course early bird menu is excellent value – with an impressive and extensive wine list. Late-night menu available after 11pm.

The Cedar Tree €€ *11a St Andrew Street, Dublin 2; Mon, Tues, Wed, Thurs, Fri & Sat 11.30am–10.30pm, Sun 1–10pm; tel: 01 677 2121; http://thecedartree.ie.* The Lebanese food here is authentic and reasonably priced, with good vegetarian options and wonderful meze dishes, wines, and even belly dancers on occasion.

Chili Club €€ *1 Anne's Lane, South Anne Street, Dublin 2; Wed, Thurs & Fri 12.30–2.30pm & 5–10pm, Sat & Sun 5–10pm; tel: 01 677 3721; www.chiliclub. ie.* One of the oldest Thai restaurants in Dublin. Good, authentic food served in a small, intimate setting. Vegetarian options available on a pleasingly extensive menu.

Cornucopia € *19–20 Wicklow Street, Dublin 2; Mon & Tues 9.30–7pm, Wed, Thurs, Fri & Sat 9.30am–8pm, Sun 10.30–8pm; tel: 01 677 7583; www.cornucopia.ie.* An informal counter service veggie place that non-vegetarians can enjoy too. Serves delicious home-cooked vegetarian and vegan meals from breakfast through to dinner.

Dax €€€€ *23 Pembroke Street Upper, Dublin 2; Tues, Wed, Thurs & Fri 12.30–2.30pm & 5.30–9pm, Sat 5.30–9pm; tel: 01 676 1494; www.dax.ie.* Dax is worth visiting for its delightful rustic and continental food with a French emphasis. Tapas is available at the bar.

Dunne & Crescenzi €€ *14–16 South Frederick Street, Dublin 2; daily 10.30am–late; tel: 01 677 3815, www.dunneandcrescenzi.com.* The tables are packed into this small but pleasantly authentic Italian joint. Everything is well prepared and big on taste. Great antipasti plates.

Fallon & Byrne €€€ *11–17 Exchequer Street, Dublin 2; daily noon–3pm, Tues 5.30–9pm, Wed & Thurs 5.30–10pm, Fri & Sat 5.30–11pm, Sun 5.30–9pm; tel: 01*

472 1000; www.fallonandbyrne.com. Fallon & Byrne's beautiful dining room makes it a particularly pleasant place to enjoy lunch or Sunday brunch. This French restaurant has good service, quality bistro cooking, and a fabulous New York-style deli downstairs – if you have any room left.

Glovers Alley by Andy McFadden €€€€ *128 Stephen's Green, Dublin 2; Thurs, Fri & Sat 12.30–2.15pm, Tues, Wed, Thurs, Fri & Sat 6–9.15pm; tel: 01 244 0733;* www.gloversalley.ie. A talented team led by chef Andy McFadden use the finest Irish ingredients to create stylish, French-influenced, contemporary food in a sophisticated setting, just a few short steps from Grafton Street and overlooking St Stephen's Green.

Il Fornaio € *1b Valentina House, Mayor Square, IFSC, Dublin 1; daily noon–10pm; tel: 01 672 1853;* www.ilfornaioifsc.ie. No frills, but there is authentic homemade Italian food at reasonable prices. The restaurant is fairly small but has outdoor tables to enjoy *alfresco* dining during better weather.

Forno 500° € *74 Dame Street, Dublin 2; daily noon–11.30pm; tel: 01 679 4555;* www.forno500.ie. This artisan Italian restaurant, bar and pizzeria specialises in genuine Neapolitan sourdough pizza baked in the first authentic fixed Neapolitan wood-fire oven (forno) in Ireland. Located next door to the Olympia Theatre Dublin, it is the perfect spot for dinner and a show.

Good World €€ *18 South Great George's Street, Dublin 2; daily 12.30–9.30pm; tel: 01 677 5373; 26 Westmoreland Street; daily 12.30pm–8pm; tel: 01 442 0024;* www.goodworld.ie. Perfect for authentic Chinese food, less geared to Western tastes, and the best dim sum in the city. For a taste of Asian street food culture visit Good World Westmoreland Street.

Izakaya and Sake Bar *12/13 South Great Georges Street, Dublin.2; Tues, Wed & Thurs 5–9.30pm; Fri 5–10pm, Sat 1–10pm, Sun 5–9.30pm; tel: 01 645 8001.* Tempura, sushi, Japanese grill, and ramen are freshly prepared daily at South and North city venues. Part of the Yamamori chain.

Kathmandu Kitchen €–€€ *18 Dame St, Dublin 2; Mon, Tues, Wed, Thurs & Fri noon–2.30pm & 5–11pm, Sat & Sun 1–10.30pm; tel: 01 6111 706; The Mall, Main Street, Malahide, Co Dublin; Mon, Wed & Thurs 4.30–10.30pm, Sun*

1–9.30pm; tel: 01 8456141; www.kathmandukitchen.ie. Serves authentic regional Nepalese and Indian cuisine with a unique blend of fresh Himalayan herbs and spices.

L'Gueuleton €€€ *1 Fade Street, Dublin 2; Mon, Tues, Wed, Thurs, Fri & Sat 12.30–11.30pm, Sun 5.30–10.00; tel: 087 939 3608,* www.lgueuleton.com. This rustic yet contemporary French restaurant serves up robust dishes with a classic bistro edge. It is hugely popular and has an undeniable charm with its rickety wooden tables and blackboards.

Lemon Crepe & Coffee Co € *66 South William Street, Dublin 2; Mon, Tues, Wed, Thurs & Fri 8am–5pm, Sat 8.30am–5pm, Sun 9.30am–5pm; tel: 01 672 9044;* www.lemonco.com. An array of sweet and savoury crepes, Belgium waffles, and pancakes. Serves a great coffee.

Market Bar €€ *Fade Street, Dublin 2; Mon–Thu noon–11.30pm, Fri–Sat until 1.30am, Sun until 11pm tel: 01 613 9094;* www.marketbar.ie. A gorgeous cavernous bar serving an exciting selection of tapas – Cajun sea trout, steamed mussels, beef stew – in small or large portions, with a good choice of wine.

Nanettis €€€ *22 Dawson Street; Mon–Fri 5–10pm, Sat 1–10pm. Closed Sun and Bank Holidays; tel: 01 662 4736;* www.nannettis.ie. Nanetti's is a new Italian resturant that is a bit of a crowd pleaser in a stylish space with brick walls and marble counters. Try the *fritto misto*, veal *saltimboca* or *gnocchi alla casa* with *tortino* or *tiramisu* to finish. Good wine list too.

Restaurant Patrick Guilbaud €€€€ *21 Upper Merrion Street, Dublin 2; Tues, Wed, Thurs, Fri & Sat 12.30–last orders 2pm & 7–last orders 9pm; tel: 01 676 4192;* www.restaurantpatrickguilbaud.ie. Set in an elegant eighteen-century townhouse adjoining the Merrion Hotel, this two Michelin star restaurant is the capital's finest French restaurant, with prices to match.

The Rustic Stone €€ *17 South Great George's Street, Dublin 2; Mon, Tues, Wed, Thurs & Fri noon–4.30pm & 5.30–10.30pm, Sat 1–11pm, Sun 2–9pm; tel: 01 707 9596;* www.rusticstone.ie. Chef Dylan McGrath prepares the finest meat and fish in tasty marinades, and guests cook it themselves at the table on a hot stone. A tempting tapas menu of healthy but indulgent bites, and a 'rustic raw' lunch menu, attract a lively and glam clientele. This is Dublin dining at its liveliest.

Saba €€€ *26–28 South William Street, Dublin 2; daily noon–10.30pm; tel: 01 679 2000;* www.sabadublin.com; *22 Upper Baggot Street, Dublin 4; 01 563 1999.* A popular Thai and Vietnamese eatery, known for its authentic menu and contemporary interior. The menu features tasty wok-based dishes, salads, noodles, and curries.

Shanahan's on the Green €€€€ *119 St Stephen's Green, Dublin 2; Tues, Wed, Thurs & Fri 5.30–10.00pm, Sat 6–10.00pm; tel: 01 407 0939;* www.shanahans. ie. Luxurious, fashionable and very expensive American steakhouse in a sumptuous Georgian decor. The certified Irish Angus beef steaks are magnificent. Good wine list, strong on California. Vegetarian menu also available for non-meat eating companions. Downstairs is the resident bar, **The Oval Office**, which features an interesting display of memorabilia related to US Presidents with Irish heritage.

The Vintage Kitchen €€ *7 Poolbeg Street, Dublin 2; Daily, noon–10pm; tel: 01 679 8705;* www.thevintagekitchen.ie. Cosy eatery specialising in Irish food made with local ingredients. Mouth-watering menus frequently change. Some vintage arts and crafts for sale. It's better to book in advance because the restaurant is rather small.

Al Vesuvio €–€€ *Meeting House Square, Temple Bar, Dublin 2; Mon, Tues, Wed & Thurs 5–10pm, Fri 4–10.30pm, Sat 1–10.30pm, Sun 2–9pm; tel: 01 671 4597;* www.alvesuviopizzeria.com. A tastebud tickling traditional Italian pizzeria and osteria perfectly positioned in Dublin's cultural quarter (ideal for pre or post-theatre/film feasting), serving pizzas (flame-baked in an open brick oven), pasta, seafood, steak, and vegetarian dishes. Portions are generous and good value.

OLD TOWN/LIBERTIES

The Fumbally € *Fumbally Lane, The Liberties, Dublin 8; Wed, Thurs, Fri 9am–3pm, Sun 10am–3pm; tel: 01 529 8732;* www.thefumbally.ie. The owner-chef co-operative gained experience cooking at festivals and travelling, and the result is a distinctly different eatery, casual and friendly. Local, organic and free-range produce is cooked with Middle Eastern and Mediterranean spices.

Leo Burdock's € *2 Werburgh Street, Christchurch, Dublin 8; Sun, Mon, Tues, Wed & Thurs 11.30am–12pm, Fri & Sat 11.30am–12pm; tel: 01 454 0306; www. leoburdock.com.* Dublin's most famous chippy, established in 1913, has no indoor seating but serves the freshest, most delicious fish and chips to take away. Franchises in Cookstown, Howth, Rathmines and Temple Bar.

Los Chicanos € *Eliot's Cash & Carry, 10 Camden Row, Saint Kevin's; Fri 6–9pm, Sat–Sun 3.30–9pm; tel: 01 661 1919; www.loschicanos.ie; hola@loschicanos. ie.* Native Irish chef Scott Holder brings the authentic flavours of Mexico to Dublin in the form of a very cool foodtruck. Order fish, chorizo, lamb, sweetpotato or cauliflower tacos, salsas and sides. Gluten free. It won't be long before there's a restaurant. Check the location in advance as it is subject to change.

Queen of Tarts € *Cows Lane, Temple Bar, Dublin 8, Wed, Thurs, Fri & Sat 9am–4pm, Sun 10am–4pm; tel: 01 633 4681; Cork Hill, Dame Street, Dublin 2; tel 01 670 7499; www.queenoftarts.ie.* Homely and welcoming, with an array of delectable pastries, cakes, and salads to delight your taste buds, this place is perfect for lunch or a light bite.

TEMPLE BAR

Elephant and Castle €€ *18–19 Temple Bar, Dublin 2; daily noon–10pm; tel: 01 533 7563; www.elephantandcastle.ie.* Good food and reasonable prices have assured the longevity of this informal place – it opened in 1989. Come here for gourmet burgers, salads and the famous spicy chicken wings. Great for families with teens and younger children. Takeaway available too and franchises city-wide.

Gallagher's Boxty House €€ *20–21 Temple Bar, Dublin 2; daily noon–9.30pm; tel: 01 677 2762, www.boxtyhouse.ie.* Boxty is an old Irish dish: potato pancakes stuffed with a variety of fillings (including vegetarian), served at long tables to traditional Irish background music; a must-visit for every tourist to the city.

CITY CENTRE NORTH

Chapter One Restaurant €€€€ *18–19 Parnell Square, Dublin 1; Tues, Wed, Thurs, Fri & Sat 6.30–9.30pm, Thurs, Fri & Sat 12.30–2pm; tel: 01 873 2266; www.chapteronerestaurant.com.* One of the city's best restaurants, set in the basement of the Dublin Writers Museum, with excellent modern Irish dishes accompanied by fine wines.

Ely Bar and Grill €€ *George's Dock, North Dock, Dublin 1; Mon, Tues, Wed, Thurs, Fri & Sat noon–10pm, Sun noon–6pm; tel: 01 672 0010; www.elywinebar.ie.* Trendy wine bar serving flame-grilled dry-aged steaks, fresh Irish seafood, and local vegetables, washed down with fine wines, Irish whiskeys, ice-cold beers, and signature cocktails.

Gallery Restaurant at the Church €€ Junction of *Mary Street and Jervis Street, Dublin 1; Mon, Tues & Wed noon–10pm, Thurs noon–11.30pm, Fri & Sat noon–12am, Sun noon–10pm; tel: 01 828 0102; www.thechurch.ie.* This is a stunning venue that comes complete with a massive church organ and stained-glass windows. An international menu with an Irish twist is served.

Yamamori – North City €€ *38–39 Ormond Quay Lower, Dublin 1; Sun. Mon. Tues & Wed noon–9pm, Thurs, Fri & Sat noon–10pm; tel: 01 872 0003;* **South City** *72 South Great George's Street, Dublin 2; tel: 01 475 5001; www.yamamori.ie.* You can't beat this Japanese favourite for its excellent tempura, ramen and sushi dishes. Overlooking the iconic Ha'penny Bridge, the location is hard to beat and the Japanese grill is pretty delicious, too.

SOUTH SUBURBS

Ananda Sandyford Road €€€€ *Dundrum Town Centre; Mon–Sat 5.30–10.45pm, also Fri–Sat 12.30–2.30pm, Sun 1–2.45pm and 5.30–9.30pm; tel: 01-296 0099; www.anandarestaurant.ie.* The intricate presentation and delicate spicing of the dishes – a wonderful *amuse-bouche* of lentil soup, a divine crab terrine and fabulous thalis – will blow you away. of the Michelin-starred Indian restaurant Benares in London. Run by Atul Kochhar, chef-patron of the Michelin-starred Indian restaurant Benares in London.

The Lobster Pot €€€€ *9 Ballsbridge Terrace, Ballsbridge, Dublin 4; Tues, Thurs, Fri & Sat 5.45–9.45pm; tel: 01 668 0025; www.thelobsterpot.ie.* This fine dining restaurant has a charming, old-world atmosphere and serves up an exquisite fish menu. Choose from the daily catch and have it cooked to your liking. Meat options are available too.

Roly's Bistro €€€ *7 Ballsbridge Terrace, Dublin 4; daily noon–3pm & 5.45–10pm; tel: 01 668 0611; www.rolysbistro.ie.* Attractive bistro restaurant on two floors, with imaginative and well-presented menus, usually focused on classic fish and meat dishes. Good service and a lively atmosphere.

OUTSIDE DUBLIN

Cavistons Seabar €€ *58 Glasthule Road, Sandycove, County Dublin; Thurs 3–8pm, Fri & Sat 1–9pm, Sun 12.30pm–7.45pm; tel: 01 223 8273; www.cavistonsseabar.com.* The quintessential end to a day by the sea; hand cut chips, and fresh hake, haddock, monkfish, or shellfish.

Jaipur €€€ *5 St James's Terrace, Malahide, Co. Dublin; Tues, Wed, Thurs, Fri & Sat 5–10pm, Sun 2–9pm; tel: 01 845 5455; 21 Castle Street, Dalkey; tel: 01 285 0552; www.jaipur.ie.* Jaipur serves modern Indian food made using seasonal Irish ingredients such as organic Wicklow lamb. Takeaway service available. Vegan friendly.

King Sitric €€€€ *East Pier, Howth, Co. Dublin; Fri & Sat 6–8.30 tel: 01 832 5235, www.kingsitric.ie;* **East Café Bar €** *Thurs, Fri, Sat, Sun & Mon 1–9pm.* A long-established fine-dining restaurant in a lovely waterside setting. Owner and Head Chef Aidan McManus is committed to sourcing fresh fish and shellfish from the boats (or his own lobster pots) and has a fine wine list. The East Café Bar, located on the ground floor, with its own terrace and beach huts, serves light bites.

Sienna's €€ *9 Marine Court, The Green, Malahide, Co Dublin; Mon, Tues, Wed, Thurs & Fri 5–10pm, Sat & Sun 1–10pm; tel: 01 845 1233; www.nautilusmalahide.ie.* Elegant and relaxed dining atmosphere in a room overlooking Malahide Marina. Beautifully presented plates of local seafood and Italian dishes served by friendly staff.

TRAVEL ESSENTIALS

PRACTICAL INFORMATION

A

ACCOMMODATION (See also Youth Hostels)

Hotels in Ireland are classified by star ratings (from one to five), and are registered and regularly inspected by Fáilte Ireland, Ireland's national tourism development authority. Fáilte Ireland publishes a list of approved hotel and guesthouse accommodation throughout Dublin, obtainable through your local tourist information office (see Tourist Information). Hotel information can also be found on the Irish Hotels Federation website www.irelandhotels.com. All tourist information offices operate an accommodation booking service, however, it is advisable to book accommodation in advance, especially if you plan to visit in the peak months of July and August.

Hotels generally offer a full range of services, including restaurants, licensed bars, currency exchange offices, gift shops, and lounges. **Guesthouses** provide more limited facilities, but are excellent value. Be aware that room prices quoted normally include the government tax (VAT) of 13.5 percent but do not always include service charges, which could add an extra ten to fifteen percent to your bill.

Details about **self-catering accommodation** in Dublin and the surrounding area can be obtained from Fáilte Ireland, which produces a complete illustrated guide. Dublin also offers a variety of college and **university accommodation** outside of term-time. Rooms and apartments at bargain rates are available on the Trinity College campus between mid-June and mid-September. For further information, contact the Accommodation Office, Trinity College, Dublin 2; tel: 01 896 1177; www.tcd.ie. University College Dublin provides a similar service. For further information, contact the Accommodation Office, UCD, Belfield, Dublin 4; tel: 01 716 1034; www.ucd.ie.

Holiday Hostels provide simple accommodation in dormitory-style rooms or shared bedrooms for visitors on a tight budget. These are open year-round. For details of hostels in Dublin, contact Fáilte Ireland. Three places you can contact directly are: *Kinlay House Dublin,* 2–12 Lord Edward Street, Dublin 2; tel: 01 679 6644; www.kinlayhouse.ie; *Independent Holiday Hostels,* 57 Lower

Gardiner Street, Dublin 1; tel: 01 836 4700; www.hostels-ireland.com; Jacobs Inn, 21–28 Talbot Place, Dublin 1; tel: 01 855 5660; https://jacobsinn.com.

AIRPORTS

Situated approximately 10km (6 miles) north of the city centre, Dublin Airport (tel: 01 944 1111; www.dublinairport.com) is Ireland's largest and busiest airport. There are two terminals: Terminal 1 (T1) is the arrival and departure point for short-haul flights; Terminal 2 (T2) serves long-haul flights. A travel information desk is located on the arrivals level in Terminal 1 if you require assistance with your onward journey. Taxi ranks are located at zone 3 and at zone 20. Aircoach (daily 3.55am–12.25am; www.aircoach.ie) – stops at zone 2 and zone 20 – and Dublin Express (4.28am–11.28pm; www.dublinexpress.ie) – stops at zone 1 and zone 21 – run regular, shuttle services to the city centre. You can purchase your ticket in advance via carriers' websites or directly from your bus driver when boarding using contactless payment. Dublin Bus (www.dublinbus.ie), the biggest public transport provider in the Greater Dublin Area, operates from zone 15 – catch the number 16 or 41 for the city centre. The latter is the cheapest option but buses run less frequently.

B

BICYCLE RENTAL

NOW TV dublinbikes (www.dublinbikes.ie) operates a self-service bike rental system. The service is accessible daily between the hours of 5am and 12.30am and bike stations are distributed throughout the city centre. You can also hire bikes from: Belfield Bike Shop (5 Cranford Centre, Stillorgan Road, Dublin 4; tel: 089 496 5308; www.belfieldbikeshop.com); Bike Stop Dublin (37 Capel Street, Dublin 1; 085 256 3211; https://bikestopdublin.com); Phoenix Park Bikes (Gate House, Chesterfield Avenue, Phoenix Park, Dublin 8; tel: 087 379 9946 and 01 679 8290; www.phoenixparkbikes.com); and Roadbikehire.ie (6 Mountain Villa, Church Road, Killiney, Co. Dublin; tel: 086 854 5654; https://roadbikehire.ie). Cycling Safaris (Belfield Bike Shop, Dublin 4; tel: 01 260 0749; www.cyclingsafaris.com) offer guided and self-guided day trips in and around

Dublin. Dublin City Council (www.dublincity.ie) has information on cycling in Dublin and the Road Safety Authority (RSA; www.rsa.ie) has advice on cycling safely and the rules of the road. Try Cycling Ireland (www.cyclingireland.ie) for route planning.

BUDGETING FOR YOUR TRIP

Dublin is relatively expensive compared to other European capitals, and accommodation and eating out can quickly eat into your budget. The following is a rough guide only:

Accommodation. A double room in a mid-range hotel in Dublin costs from about €100 upwards per room, but you will find most places hovering around the €150 mark. Five-star hotels can easily set you back three or four times this amount. There are plenty of inexpensive accommodation options if you are prepared to look around.

Meals and drinks. Stopping off for a coffee in Dublin can often be expensive at around €2.50 to €3 for a cappuccino or latte. Drinks in bars and pubs are expensive and nowhere more so than in hotels. In city centre pubs you will pay around €5 for a pint of lager, while a spirit and a mixer can set you back around €7. Guinness usually costs upwards from around €4.50 a pint. Most restaurants are mid-range with main courses around €20 and upwards.

Entertainment. Cinema tickets costs around €10 depending on location, time, and any discounts you may be entitled to; admission to a nightclub is usually upward of €10. Many museums and galleries have free admission making sightseeing a relatively cheap option.

Transport. The best deal travellers can get for travelling around Dublin is a Leap Visitor Card (https://about.leapcard.ie). These allow unlimited travel on all Dublin Bus scheduled services, Go-Ahead Ireland city services, Luas (tram) services, DART (Dublin Area Rapid Transport) and Commuter Rail services in Dublin city and county for a specified time period – one (€10), three (€19.50) or seven days (€40). Your chosen time period activates when you first use the card. Cards can be purchased at Dublin Airport at the travel information desk, Spar and WHSmith.

Specials: The DoDublin Freedom Card (https://dodublin.ie) combines the

Leap Visitor Card (valid for 72 hours) with DoDublin Hop-On Hop-Off City Tour (valid for 48 hours). An adult ticket costs €45. The Dublin Pass digital ticket (https://dublinpass.com) includes free entry to over thirty top tourist attractions and a guidebook. Passes are available for one, two, three, four, and five days. Prices start at €70 for an adult day pass.

C

CAR HIRE (See also Driving)

Driving in the city is difficult, but it is worth hiring a car to explore the surrounding countryside. You can arrange to hire a car immediately upon arrival at the airport, or have one waiting for you if you book a fly-drive or rail-sail-drive inclusive package. To hire a car, you will need a driving licence issued in your home country, valid for at least two to five years. The minimum age (usually from twenty-three to twenty-five) varies from company to company, and most do not rent to those over seventy or seventy-five. Rates include third-party liability insurance, and sometimes collision damage waiver (CDW) but check for excess liabilities. The cost of hiring a medium-sized car for one day in Dublin can range upwards of €140 in February to €250 in August.

Major car hire companies:

Avis, Dublin Airport, Terminal 1 Arrivals and the multi-storey car park in Terminal 2; tel: 01 605 7500; www.avis.ie; 39 Old Kilmainham Road, Dublin 8; tel: 01 605 7501.

Budget, Dublin Airport, Terminal 1 and 2 Arrivals; tel: 01 844 5150; www.budget.ie; 151 Lower Drumcondra Road, Dublin 9; tel: 01 837 9611.

Hertz, Dublin Airport, Terminal 1 and 2 Arrivals; tel: 01 844 5466, www.hertz.ie.

National, Dublin Airport, Terminal 2 Arrivals; tel: 01 844 5848; www.nationalcar.com.

Dan Dooley, Dublin Airport, Terminal 1 and 2 Arrivals; tel: 01 844 5151; www.dan-dooley.ie.

CLIMATE

Dublin's has a temperate climate without extremes of temperature, thanks to the warming Gulf Stream that influences much of the country. The weather is unpredictable and can change very quickly from rain to sun (and vice versa) due to blustery winds coming in from the Irish Sea. However, less rain falls on Dublin than on any other part of the country and snow is a rare occurrence. Summers can be quite cool and days can be unexpectedly warm in winter.

	J	F	M	A	M	J	J	A	S	O	N	D
°C	7	8	11	13	16	18	20	21	17	14	11	8
°F	45	46	52	55	61	64	68	70	63	57	52	46

CLOTHING

Dubliners are fashion-conscious, and a certain standard of attire is expected in exclusive hotels and restaurants. Business people still dress in formal dark suits. For everyday wear, however, jeans and casual clothes are appropriate. A raincoat or umbrella is an absolute necessity. If you plan to walk a lot, especially in the environs of Dublin, bring sturdy shoes and a sweater – even if it looks like a glorious day, it can turn cold later on. Pack warm clothing for winter, and a jacket and sweater in summer. Evening temperatures on the sunniest summer days can be quite cool; in spring there is often a cool breeze that adds an edge to the day's mild warmth.

CRIME AND SAFETY (See also Emergencies)

Compared to most urban centres, Dublin's crime rate is moderate, and violent street crime is rare. Unfortunately, crime is on the increase. Be wary of pickpockets in pubs or crowded places. Avoid Phoenix Park after dark.

If you are robbed, report the incident to the hotel receptionist and the nearest police station so that the police can provide you with a certificate to present to your insurance company. Call your consulate if your passport has been stolen. Tourist information offices and some attractions provide a multilingual leaflet produced by the Garda (see Police), entitled *A Short Guide to Tourist Security*. The Irish Tourist Assistance Service (Pearse Street Garda Station, Pearse Street, Dublin 2; tel: 01 666 9354; www.itas.ie) is there to provide support and information to tourists who have been the victim of a crime or traumatic event.

D

DRIVING

Road Conditions. If you must drive in the city centre, avoid the worst congestion by travelling between 10am and 4pm. Outside the city, the motorway system offers rapid transit. However, the most scenic routes, such as those through the Wicklow Mountains, tend to be narrow, winding and steep.

Rules and Regulations. Traffic follows the same basic rules that apply in Britain. Drive on the left and overtake on the right. Turn left on a roundabout; at a junction where no road has priority, yield to traffic coming from the right. Road signs giving place directions are bilingual, in Irish and English, and distances are shown in kilometres. Seat belts in both the front and back must be worn, and children under-12 must travel in the rear. Ireland has very strict rules about drinking and driving – don't do it. The Road Safety Authority (RSA; https://www.rsa.ie) provides advice for tourists driving in Ireland, you can download a tourists' guide from their website.

Petrol (gas). There are filling stations everywhere, many of them open 24 hours. Petrol is dispensed from the green-handled nozzle: the black one is for diesel.

Parking. It is almost impossible to find free parking on Dublin's streets during normal working hours, but you may have better luck at weekends. Expect to be towed away or heavily fined for parking illegally. Metered parking (for up to 2 hours) is quite limited. Your safest bet is to park in one of the multi-storey car parks (prices vary).

Speed limits. The speed limit is 50kph in towns and cities, 80kph on regional and local roads and 100kph on national roads. On motorways the speed limit is 120kph.

If You Need Help. If you are a member of an AIT driving club or the AA, call the Automobile Association of Ireland (tel: 01 617 9999 or emergency 1800 66 77 88). The Royal Automobile Club (RAC) also has a breakdown number (toll-free: 1800 535005).

E

ELECTRICITY
Ireland's electrical supply is 220 volts 50 hertz and three-pin plugs and two-pin (110 volts to 120 volts) plugs are used. If you need a travel adaptor, bring one with you.

EMBASSIES AND CONSULATES
Australia: 47–49 St Stephen's Green, Dublin 2; tel: (01) 664 5300; www.ireland.embassy.gov.au
Canada: 7–8 Wilton Terrace, Dublin 2; tel: (01) 234 4000; www.canada.ie
Great Britain: 29 Merrion Road, Dublin 4; tel: (01) 205 3700; www.britishembassyinireland.fco.gov.uk
US: 42 Elgin Road, Dublin 4; tel: (01) 668 8777; https://ie.usembassy.gov
For a full list of Foreign Embassies in Ireland visit https://www.dfa.ie/embassies.

EMERGENCIES (See also Health and Medical Care and Police)
In the event of an emergency, dial 999 or 112 toll-free for Police, Ambulance, Fire and Coastguard.

G

GETTING THERE (See Airports)
All visitors should check the latest travel advice in place before travel.
By Air. Aer Lingus (www.aerlingus.com), Ireland's national airline, operates short-haul flights to Dublin from points in the UK and Europe and long-haul flights from Australia, North America, and the United Arab Emirates. Depending on your point of origin you may need to make a layover and catch a con-

necting flight. Ryanair (www.ryanair.com) operates budget flights to Dublin from points in France, Greece, Italy, Portugal, Ukraine, the UK, and Spain.

Holiday packages that include accommodation generally offer the best rates and conditions. A wide range of package tours or special-interest holidays are available, including fly-drive, sporting and activity holidays, and short breaks.

By Bus. Bus Éireann (Busárus, Central Bus Station, Store Street; tel: 01 836 6111; www.buseireann.ie; https://eurolines.buseireann.ie), Ireland's national bus company, operates a daily Eurolines coach service between Ireland and the UK via Expressway and National Express. Sailings with Irish Ferries are through Dublin, Holyhead, Rosslare and Pembroke. Bus Éireann also provides countrywide bus services.

By Ferry. Two main ferry companies service Ireland. Irish Ferries (tel: 01 204 777; https://www.irishferries.com) sails from Holyhead to Dublin Port, Pembroke to Rosslare, and Cherbourg to Dublin. Stena Line (01 204 7777; www.stenaline.co.uk) sails from Holyhead to Dublin, Fishguard to Rosslare, Cairnryan to Belfast, and Liverpool to Belfast.

GUIDED TOURS

Bus Tours. The DoDublin Hop On Hop Off Tour (https://dodublin.ie) provides an excellent introduction to Dublin. The tour starts at Dublin Bus Head Office, 59 Upper O'Connell Street, and takes in the principal sights; in good weather, the tour is by open-top bus. The Fáilte Ireland trained bus-drivers/tour guides are entertaining, sometimes there is a singsong, and you can hop on or off at any of the stops. DoDublin also provide pre-recorded multilingual tours (Irish, English, French, German, Spanish, Italian, Russian, Portuguese and Chinese). DoDublin also offer an amusing, offbeat Ghostbus Tour (for younger visitors there is a Ghostbus Kids Tour) and several Day Tours from Dublin. Tickets can be purchased on DoDublin website, at the Bus and Travel Information Desk at Dublin airport or at Dublin Bus Head Office.

Bus Éireann runs day trips out of the city to sights such as Glendalough, Newgrange, and the Boyne Valley, Wicklow and Powerscourt Gardens, as well as further afield. All tours depart from Busáras (22 Store St, North Dock, Dublin

1) (see page 128). Irish Day Tours (37 College Green, Dublin 2; tel: 01 907 3265, www.irishdaytours.ie) and Gray Line Ireland Tours (118 Grafton Street, Dublin 2; tel: 01 685 4045, www.graylineireland.com) offers a range of excursions from Dublin.

Walking Tours. If you feel up for a challenge, search the city for vinyl record-shaped plaques. These are the remnants of the now obsolete Rock 'n' Stroll Trail. Plaques are displayed on several buildings and mark places associated with famous musical artists such as Bob Geldof, U2, and the Chieftains.

Follow in the footsteps of Dublin's famous wordsmiths, the enjoyable Dublin Literary Pub Crawl (tel: 01 670 5602; www.dublinpubcrawl.com) comprises of an evening of readings, song, and performance, and a private visit to Trinity College.

Historical Walking Tours of Dublin (tel: 087 688 9412; www.historicaltours.ie) offer a series of informative and entertaining themed walks that run the gamut from architecture to Vikings.

The Traditional Irish Musical Pub Crawl (tel: 01 475 3313; www.discover-dublin.ie) is led by a couple of professional musicians – they play, sing, and talk about the history of Irish music.

Pat Liddy's Walking Tours (tel: 01 832 9406; www.walkingtours.ie) cover the highlights of Dublin's literary locations, Georgian architecture, and the city's hidden corners. Tickets can be booked online or at the Dublin Bus Head Office.

The International Bar on Wicklow Street is the starting point for the daily 1916 Rebellion Walking Tour (tel: 086 858 3847; www.1916rising.com); discover the sites of the Easter Rising.

Sandemans New Europe excellent, bilingual (English and Spanish) Free Dublin Tour (www.newdublintours.com) leaves from City Hall at 11am for a three-hour-long, tips-only jaunt around the city.

H

HEALTH AND MEDICAL CARE

Visitors from EU/EEA and Switzerland can use a valid European Health Insurance Card (EHIC) to access necessary medical treatment free of charge in Ireland. EHIC only covers public healthcare. For UK citizens an existing EHIC will remain valid until the expiry date on the card. The UK Global Health Insurance Card (UK GHIC) has replaced the EHIC for most people. If you are visiting from outside these areas, you may wish to consider taking out travel insurance.

In the event of an accident, dial 999 or 112 toll-free for an ambulance. Your hotel or guesthouse proprietor will contact a doctor in an emergency. Beaumont Hospital (Beaumont Road, Dublin 9; tel: 01 809 3000) has a 24-hour emergency room. For non-emergency services, try the Grafton Medical (34 Grafton Street; Mon, Tues, Wed, Thurs & Fri 9am–5pm; tel: 01 671 2122).

If you need emergency dental treatment, call the Irish Dental Association (Unit 2, Leopardstown Office Park, Sandyford, Dublin 8; tel: 01 295 0072; www.dentist.ie), which will be able to recommend a dentist.

Pharmacies are generally open during normal business hours. You can find the address of the nearest late-night pharmacy in the local press and under 'Chemists – Pharmaceutical' in the phone directory. There is a branch of Boots on Grafton Street. Pharmacies on O'Connell Street tend to stay open quite late. Pharmacies also open on a Sunday.

If you have any symptoms of COVID-19 (coronavirus), self-isolate and get a COVID-19 test even if you are part or fully vaccinated against COVID-19. Call 112 or 999 if you are very short of breath and cannot complete a sentence.

HOLIDAYS

Shops, banks, official departments, and restaurants are closed on public holidays. If a holiday falls on a Sunday, the following Monday is normally taken instead. The ban on selling alcohol in pubs on Good Friday was rescinded in 2018.

1 January: New Year's Day
17 March: St Patrick's Day
25 December: Christmas Day
26 December: St Stephen's Day
Movable Dates
February, March, and April: Ash Wednesday/Easter Monday

First Monday in June: Whit or June Bank Holiday
First Monday in August: August Bank Holiday
November 2 or November 3: All Souls' Day

L

LANGUAGE

Ireland is officially bilingual, and on official occasions either English or Irish may be used. English is spoken in Dublin and throughout most of Ireland; Irish is the primary language in areas designated as *Gaeltacht*. Irish is a required school subject, so most Irish people have some knowledge of it. Signs around Dublin are usually self-explanatory but road signs throughout the country feature place names in both languages. On buses, *An Lár* means 'City Centre'. Often seen on toilet doors (sometimes without pictorial explanation), '*Fir*' is the 'Mens' (litterally 'man') and '*Mná*' is the 'Ladies', (litterally 'woman').

LGBTQ TRAVELLERS

Ireland in general has a progressive and positive outlook towards the LGBTQ community and it was the first country in the world to legalise same-sex marriage by public vote in November 2016. As such, the LGBTQ community is both visible and welcoming to visitors, especially in the larger cities. The monthly newspaper, *Gay Community News* (www.gcn.ie) is widely available, and there are listings and features in many of Dublin's free magazines and papers. Annual LGBTQ events include the Dublin Gay Theatre Festival (May), Pride (June), and the GAZE International LGBTQ+ Film Festival (Irish Film Institute, August). Good bars and nightclubs include the long-standing The George (89 South Great George's Street), Street 66 (33–34 Parliament Street) and Pantibar (7–8 Capel Street).

Help and information lines include The Switchboard – LGBTQIA Support & Resources (tel: 01 872 1055; www.theswitchboard.ie) and Lesbian Line (tel: 01 872 9911; www.dublinlesbianline.ie). Outhouse (105 Capel Street, Dublin 2; tel: 01 873 4999; www.outhouse.ie) is a LGBTQ community and resource centre.

M

MAPS

You can purchase detailed maps of Dublin and its environs in bookshops. If you need less detail, tourist offices have free tourist maps.

MEDIA

Radio and TV. Raidió Teilifís Éireann (RTÉ) is Ireland's national television and radio broadcaster and runs four TV channels, RTÉ1, RTÉ2, RTÉjr, and RTÉ News Now and four FM radio stations, RTÉ Radio 1, RTÉ 2FM, RTÉ Raidió na Gaeltachta and RTÉ Lyric FM. TG4 is an Irish language television station. TV3, 3e and Be3 have been rebranded as Virgin Media One, Two and Three. Television programmes from Britain via the BBC and ITV (independent television) are also available, as well as all the BBC radio stations. Many hotels are equipped to receive satellite television or cable via Sky TV and other operators.

Newspapers and Magazines. The *Irish Times* is the leading national daily, with interesting articles and a useful Notices section. The *Irish Independent* has more Ireland focused coverage and publishes a special Sunday edition. The *Evening Herald*, hawked at numerous street corners, is Dublin's local tabloid, with an extensive Classifieds section. In the morning, watch out for Herald AM and Metro, which are given out free at DART stations. Most newsagents stock the main UK national dailies, plus Irish editions of English papers such as the *Sunday Times*, and many sell American and European newspapers. Foreign newspapers and periodicals can be purchased at Easons (40–42 Lower O'Connell Street).

For what's going on, try *Totally Dublin* (www.totallydublin.ie), an events listings magazine and website.

MONEY

Currency. Ireland's monetary unit is the euro (€), which is divided into 100 cents (¢). Banknotes are issued in €5, €10, €20, €50, €100, €200 and €500 denominations. Coins come in denominations of 1¢, 2¢, 5¢, 10¢, 20¢ and 50¢

and €1 and €2.

Changing money. For the best exchange rate, visitors should use banks, post offices, and bureaux de change. The best rates are often obtained by using a credit card. Note that the Bank of Ireland ATMs charge for transactions with foreign banks.

Credit cards and travellers' cheques. Visa and MasterCard credit/debit cards are widely accepted. American Express cards are only accepted in some places. Some guesthouses may not accept credit cards, so be sure to ask before booking. Traveller's cheques are no longer widely used and most banks will not accept them.

OPENING HOURS

Banks are usually open weekdays from 10am to 4pm Monday to Friday; nearly all are open at lunchtime.

Most stores follow Dublin's normal opening hours: Monday–Saturday 9am–6pm, with late night shopping on Thursday until 8pm. A few suburban shopping centres stay open until 9pm on Thursday or Friday. In tourist areas hours are usually extended, and most places in Grafton Street remain open well into the evening and on Sunday. Most supermarkets are open late until 10pm on weekdays.

Most pubs are open all day from 10.30am to 12.30am, with a slightly later opening on Sunday, and earlier closing in winter. Many pubs in the city centre stay open until 1.30am or later from Thursday to Saturday.

Note that shops cannot sell alcohol before 12 noon on Sundays.

POLICE

Ireland's national police force is An Garda Síochána. In an emergency dial 999 or 112 toll-free. For non-emergency or general enquiries, contact your nearest Garda Station.

POST OFFICES

Post office branches are open Monday to Friday 9am to 5.30pm, and Saturday 9am to 1pm. There is a post office at Dublin Airport, a convenient branch is near the tourist office on St Andrew Street and there is a branch on Merrion Row close to the museums and St Stephen's Green. Mailboxes are painted green and have the word 'Post' in yellow on the top.

Dublin's main post office is the General Post Office (GPO) on O'Connell Street. It is open from 8am to 6pm Monday to Saturday. Many post offices exchange foreign currency.

PUBLIC TRANSPORT

Bus. Dublin Bus (Bus Átha Cliath) operates the city's bus network. The company is a subsidiary of the national transport company, CIE. The head office is at 59 O'Connell Street, Dublin 1 (tel: 01 873 4222; www.dublinbus.ie). Their yellow and blue single and double deckers serve the city and the Greater Dublin area. Buses run from 6am–11.30pm. On popular routes, buses run every ten to twenty minutes, but service on other routes is less frequent. There is a special half-hourly Nitelink service to the suburbs from midnight–4am Friday and Saturday (buses depart from College, D'Olier and Westmoreland streets every half hour; buy your tickets in advance at the stops or pay on the bus with coins only; €5). A frequent bus service links Heuston Station and Busáras with Dublin airport. You need to have the right change ready unless you have a special pass (see below), which should be inserted into the reader as you enter the bus on the right-hand side (combined bus/DART tickets should be shown to the driver/conductor). If you over-pay, the driver will print you a credit slip. Collect these and they will refund your money at the headquarters on O'Connell Street.

Fares. There are no flat fares on public transport, and the amount you pay depends on where you want to go. For €5 you can buy a Leap card (www.leapcard.ie), and top it up in multiples of €5, using it to pay your fare to the bus driver (it is not a swipe card), avoiding the need to carry a stash of small change. It can also be used on the Luas tram. A range of discount passes are available for bus or combined bus-and-rail. The one-day adult bus ticket allows unlimited travel on all Dublin Bus services, except Nitelink. The one-day and three-day short-hop bus/rail tickets allow unlimited transport on Dublin Bus and the DART for one person (excluding Nitelink), while the family one-day ticket extends the same concessions to two adults and up to four children under the age of sixteen. Combination bus and Luas tram tickets are also available. Seven-day passes are also available for unlimited travel on the bus. There are also a variety of student and children's passes. Passes can be obtained from the Dublin Bus Head Office or from any bus ticket agent.

Luas Tram. The Luas tram (tel: 1800 300 604 toll-free in Ireland; www.luas.ie) is Dublin's Light Rail Transit system, connecting the city centre with outlying suburbs. There are two lines that operate weekdays from 5.30am to 12.30am, Saturday 6.30am to 12.30am and Sunday 7am to 11.30pm. The Red Line runs from The Point to Tallaght (and Saggart) every ten to twelve minutes, with stops at Connolly Station, Four Courts, Smithfield, the National Museum, and Heuston Station. The cross-city Green Line runs from Brides Glen to Broombridge – with a loop around the city centre and stops at places including St Stephen's Green, O'Connell Street, Parnell, Abbey Street, and Trinity – every five to fifteen minutes. Single fares range from €2.10 to €3.20 depending on the distance travelled (cheaper with a Leap Card). All stops have ticket machines. Return tickets, one-day, and seven-day tickets are also available.

Rail/DART. Dublin Area Rapid Transit (DART, www.irishrail.ie) provides a swift and efficient electrified rail link through the city, from the seaside towns of Howth and Malahide in the north and Greystones in the south. The line runs along the Dublin Bay coast and serves a total of thirty stations. Trains run approximately every fifteen minutes (every five minutes during rush hours) from 5.30am to midnight Monday to Saturday, and from 9am to 11.30pm on Sunday. Avoid travelling at peak times when trains are packed with commuters. Single fares range from €2.10 to €4.90 (cheaper with a Leap Card; daily and weekly tickets also available).

Taxi. You'll find taxis at one of the many clearly marked taxi ranks located outside major hotels, bus and railway stations, and on busy thoroughfares. Taxis do not normally cruise for business. There are 24-hour taxi ranks at Aston Quay, College Green, O'Connell Street, Eden Quay, Grafton Street Lower, and

St Stephen's Green (North). At busy times there can be a long wait. You can also order a taxi by calling a specific company; look in the Golden Pages of the telephone directory under 'Taxicabs'.

Rates are fixed by law and displayed in all taxis. See www.transportforireland.ie for a fare estimator. They are valid for a 16km (10-mile) radius outside the city; beyond that, fares should be negotiated in advance with the driver.

T

TELEPHONES

The area code for Dublin area when calling from outside the county is 01; the country code for Ireland is 353. For directory enquires dial 11811. Direct-dial local and international calls can be made from all hotels and most guesthouses or from any public phone. Bear in mind that any calls made from a hotel will have a hefty surcharge.

To make a call within Dublin from a landline, you only need to dial the seven-digit number without the area code. To call Dublin from elsewhere in Ireland, ensure to dial the area code plus the seven-digit number. The access number for international calls is 00, followed by the country code. Pay-phone international calls are cheaper after 6pm on weekdays and at any time over the weekend. Though there are still some coin phones in existence, telephone calling cards are widely used; you can buy them in units of ten, twenty, fifty or hundred from post offices, newsstands or shops displaying a phone card notice.

If you are visiting from an EU member state your calls, texts, and data services will be charged at your home country's domestic rates. Visitors are advised to check with their mobile provider if surcharges will be applied as EU rules on roaming charges no longer apply. For visitors from outside the EU the best way to avoid high roaming charges is to buy an Irish pay-as-you-go sim card for your phone for use while in the country.

TIME ZONES

Ireland uses Greenwich Mean Time (GMT) and Irish Standard Time (IST). The clocks change biannually. The clocks go forward an hour on the last Sunday in March (IST) and go back an hour on the last Sunday in October (GMT). GMT is one hour behind Central European Time (CET). Ireland's latitude means that summer days are long – it stays light until around 11pm – and as such, daylight hours in mid-winter are likewise relatively short (it gets dark by 4pm).

New York	**Dublin**	Paris	Jo'burg	Sydney
7am	**noon**	1pm	2pm	10pm

TIPPING

Hotel bills usually include a service charge. If a service charge is included in a restaurant bill, tipping is not obligatory. If you are unsure whether a service charge has been added, ask; if not, give ten–twelve percent. Give your hairdresser/barber about ten–twelve percent; porters €1–2 per bag; taxi drivers ten–twelve percent.

TOILETS

Dublin is not well provided with public conveniences. Around Grafton Street, the shopping centres and Marks & Spencer have toilets on their top floors; there are toilets downstairs in the Trinity College Arts Building inside the Nassau Street gate. Use the facilities in museums, department stores or pubs. Toilets may be labelled with symbols, or with the words *Fir* for men and *Mná* for women.

TOURIST INFORMATION

Fáilte Ireland (The Tourism Development Authority)

General enquiries: Fáilte Ireland, 88–95 Amiens Street Dublin 1; tel: 01 884 7700; www.failteireland.ie.

Tourist information for visitors within Ireland; tel: 1850 230 330; www.discov-

erireland.ie
Tourist information for overseas visitors; www.ireland.com.

Fáilte Ireland Official Tourist Offices Dublin City:

Discover Ireland Information Centre, 14 Upper O'Connell Street, Dublin 1; tel: 01 605 7700; www.discoverireland.ie.

Visit Dublin Centre, 25 Suffolk Street, Dublin 2; tel: 01 605 7700; www.visit-dublin.com.

Tourism Ireland Offices Abroad

Australia: Level 16/109 Pitt Street, Sydney NSW 2000, Australia; tel: 029 964 6900; www.ireland.com.

Canada: 2 Bloor Street West, Suite 3403, Toronto, Ontario M4W 3E2; tel: 416 925 6368; www.ireland.com.

UK: Nations House, 103 Wigmore Street, London W1U 1QS; tel: 207 518 0800; www.ireland.com.

US: 345 Park Avenue, New York, NY 10154; tel: 212 418 0800; www.ireland.com

TRAVELLERS WITH DISABILITIES

Some historic buildings and museums do not provide wheelchair access. A facilities and accessibility guide, and fact sheets can be obtained for free from Fáilte Ireland. Other useful contacts are the National Disability Authority (tel: 01 608 0400; www.nda.ie) and the Irish Wheelchair Association (tel: 01 818 6400; www.iwa.ie).

V

VISAS

Citizens of an EU/EEA member state, Switzerland, UK, Australia, Canada, New Zealand, South Africa and the US do not require a visa to travel to Ireland. If you are from a visa required country you will need to apply for a short stay 'C' visit visa. The maximum stay allowed under a short stay 'C' visa is ninety days. Extended validity on your passport will also be necessary in order to obtain a visa.

W

WEBSITES AND INTERNET ACCESS

Information on the web can help you prepare for your trip to Dublin. You can make hotel, guesthouse or B&B reservations at www.visitdublin.com. The Irish Hotels Federation has a site at www.irelandhotels.com, and B&Bs can be booked at https://ireland-bnb.com/. For the increasingly popular option of an Airbnb, search www.airbnb.ie.

For sightseeing and other general information visit www.ireland.com, the official marketing website of Fáilte Ireland's tourism partner – Tourism Ireland. The official tourist website for Dublin is www.visitdublin.com. The Office of Public Works (OPW) also has a website: www.heritageireland.ie. These will help you plan your holiday. To see what's going on try www.entertainmentireland.ie. Free Wi-Fi access is available in many cafés, and most hotels offer guests free internet access. Most hotels and hostels have a computer available for guests to access the internet. Dublin Airport has pay-as-you-go internet kiosks.

Y

YOUTH HOSTELS

Independent Holiday Hostels of Ireland operate hostels throughout Ireland. Their headquarters are at 57 Lower Gardiner St, Dublin 1; tel: 01-836 4700; www.hostels-ireland.com.

WHERE TO STAY

There is often little difference between hotels and guesthouses in Dublin, but the latter are usually cheaper, while city centre hotels, especially in Temple Bar and in the heart of Dublin 2, tend to be noisier given the number of bars in the vicinity.

Listed below is a selection of hotels in four price categories, grouped in the following areas: Dublin city centre, north suburbs, south suburbs, and the south coast. Although the tourist information offices at O'Connell Street and Suffolk Street do offer hotel booking facilities, it is advisable to book your accommodation well in advance.

Many hotels, mostly in the top of the range, add a service charge to the quoted price, and rates shoot up during special events. To avoid any unexpected surprises, be sure to clarify what is included in the quoted rates: ask about VAT (government tax), any extra charges, and breakfast (after a full Irish breakfast you probably won't need much of a lunch). Also ask about weekend rates and other special offers or check on the hotel's website.

As a basic guide to room prices, we have used the following symbols for a double room with en suite bath or shower, usually including breakfast, service charge and tax:

€€€€	over 190 euros
€€€	140–190uros
€€	90–140 euros
€	below 90 euros

CITY CENTRE

Arlington Hotel O'Connell Bridge € *23–25 Bachelors Walk, Dublin 1, tel: 01 804 9100*, www.arlington.ie. Sensationally located 3-star hotel and pub on the north bank of the Liffey, in the absolute heart of the city, near O'Connell Bridge – handy for concert arenas, sightseeing, and theatres. Friendly staff and well-maintained rooms. The pub downstairs (facing the river) hosts Celtic Nights with live traditional Irish music and dancing. 131 rooms.

Blooms Hotel € *3–6 Anglesea Street, Temple Bar, Dublin 2, tel: 01 671 5622,* www.blooms.ie. A convenient modern hotel in the Temple Bar area, Blooms is a decent choice for partygoers, but not for those planning a quiet night. Club M Nightclub is downstairs. 100 rooms.

Brooks Hotel €€ *59–62 Drury Street, Dublin 2, tel: 01 670 4000,* www.brookshotel.ie. With a great location just a short walk from Dublin's Grafton Street, Brooks is a smart choice in the centre of the city. Rooms are spacious and comfortable. Flat screen TVs in all rooms. 98 rooms.

Buswells Hotel €€ *23–27 Molesworth Street, Dublin 2, tel: 01 614 6500,* www.buswells.ie. Centrally located in a former Georgian townhouse, Buswells has an old-world atmosphere and period furnishings. The bar is popular with politicians. 67 rooms.

Castle Hotel €€ *Gardiner Row/Great Denmark Street, Dublin 1, tel: 01 874 6949,* www.castle-hotel.ie. The Castle Hotel consists of nine tastefully restored Georgian townhouses, close to Parnell Square. Period features and decor combined with modern comforts. Small conference facilities and parking. 130 rooms.

Central Hotel €€ *1–5 Exchequer Street, Dublin 2, tel: 01 679 7302,* www.centralhoteldublin.ie. A modest and comfortable hotel, furnished in Victorian style, well-located midway between Temple Bar and Grafton Street. First floor Library Bar attracts literary types. 70 rooms.

Clarence Hotel €€€ *6–8 Wellington Quay, Dublin 2, tel: 01 407 0800,* www.theclarence.ie. Each room is uniquely designed in a contemporary style in this handsome boutique hotel, built in 1852. Adjacent to Temple Bar but set apart from the real hustle and bustle, the hotel overlooks the River Liffey. It has a lovely interior and fusion restaurant, Cleaver East. 58 rooms and suites, one penthouse suite.

Clayton Hotel Liffey Valley € *Fonthill Road, Liffey Valley, Dublin 22, tel: 01 625 8000,* www.claytonhotelliffeyvalley.com. A functional family friendly hotel in Clondalkin, 10km (6 miles) from the city centre, with a pool, and parking available at Dublin Clarion. 352 rooms.

Conrad Dublin €€€€ *Earlsfort Terrace, Dublin 2, tel: 01 602 8900,* www.hilton. com/en/conrad. Situated just off St Stephen's Green, this glass construction opposite the National Concert Hall houses one of Ireland's few five-star hotels. The Conrad's brasserie, cocktail bar and the cosy Terrace Kitchen & Social make it difficult to leave. 191 rooms and 15 suites.

Davenport Hotel €€€€ *8–10 Merrion Street Lower, Dublin 2, tel: 01 607 3500,* https://www.ocallaghancollection.com/the-davenport-dublin-ireland/. The neoclassical style of the impressive facade of this elegant 1860s building is carried over into its vast atrium lobby. Fine-dining restaurant, bar, conference facilities, car park. 102 rooms and 12 suites.

The Dean €€ € *33 Harcourt Street, Saint Kevin's, Dublin 2 tel: 01 607 8110,* https://deandublin.ie. One of Dublin's coolest hotels, high-design, comfy beds, rainfall showers, full stocked mini SMEGs, and an Instagram-worthy 360-degree view of Dublin from the rooftop bar and restaurant. 51 rooms.

Fitzsimons Hotel €€ *21–22 Wellington Quay, Dublin 2, tel: 01 677 9315,* www. fitzsimonshotel.com. If you're coming to Dublin to experience a weekend you'll soon forget, then this is the place for you. A huge nightclub and four bars over five floors make this place somewhat of an all-night affair. By day, the Millennium Bridge provides convenient access to the city's best shopping areas. 22 rooms.

Fitzwilliam Hotel €€€€ *St Stephen's Green, Dublin 2, tel: 01 478 7000,* www.fitzwilliamhotel.com. This modern, upmarket hotel is located on the Green and has a contemporary and understated elegance. There are views of Dublin from the lovely roof garden. Dine in the sophisticated and glamorous Glovers Alley by Andy McFadden. 139 rooms.

The Grafton Hotel €€€ *Stephen's Street Lower, Dublin 2, tel: 01 648 1100,* www.the-grafton-hotel.com. Formerly the Grafton Capital Hotel, this refurbished hotel reopened its doors in late 2019 having been given a €20 million facelift by the Mandrake Collection. With design influences from the 1920s, the hotel also has a chic late lounge, The Scaredy Cat. it's very centrally located and close to all the city's top attractions, as well as restaurants and bars. 127 rooms.

Gresham Hotel €€€ *23 Upper O'Connell Street, Dublin 1, tel: 01 874 6881,* www.gresham-hotels-dublin.com. One of Dublin's legendary hotels, the Gresham is based in the heart of the city, near the General Post Office. The fine, early nineteenth-century building, with its marble floors, Waterford Crystal chandeliers, and large rooms offers luxurious accommodation. 323 rooms and suites.

Maldron Hotel Smithfield €€ *The Plaza, Smithfield, Dublin 7, tel: 01 485 0900,* www.maldronhotelsmithfield.com. There are fine views of the city from the floor-to-ceiling windows in the rooms at the front of this contemporary hotel. The hotel is in the legal district behind the Four Courts, so nights are quiet. Temple Bar is just across the river and O'Connell Street is a short stroll away. 92 rooms and suites.

The Marker Hotel €€€€ *Grand Canal Square, Docklands, Dublin 2, tel: 01 687 5100,* www.themarkerhoteldublin.com. Six floors of iconic architecture and interior design situated in the heart of the futuristic docklands development area. Rooftop lounge, spa, 23m infinity pool, and all-day indoor-outdoor brasserie. 187 rooms.

Merrion Hotel €€€€ *Upper Merrion Street, Dublin 2, tel: 01 603 0600,* www.merrionhotel.com. This elegant five-star hotel encompasses four Georgian townhouses. Its gracious setting, discreet service, and beautifully-appointed rooms and suites offer an outstanding experience. One of Dublin's most notable restaurants, the 2-star Michelin restaurant, Restaurant Patrick Guilbaud (see page 109) is located here. 142 rooms and suites.

The Mont Hotel €€€ *1–4 Merrion Street Lower, Dublin 2, tel: 01 607 3800,* www.ocallaghancollection.com/the-mont-dublin-ireland. An attractive hotel with a traditional club-like feel, set in a Georgian building on the lovely Merrion Square. Convenient for the National Art Gallery, Trinity College and other attractions. Restaurant, bar, car park. 96 rooms and 2 suites.

The Morgan €€€ *10 Fleet Street, Temple Bar, Dublin 2, tel: 01 643 7000,* www.themorgan.com. The most stylish boutique hotel in Temple Bar. You should stay here if you want a romantic getaway or if you want to live it up. You can start in the chic cocktail bar, which also serves tapas. 168 rooms and suites.

Morrison Hotel €€€€ *Ormond Quay, Dublin 1, tel: 01 887 2400,* www.morrisonhotel.ie. One of Dublin's most sophisticated hotels, set in a modern building overlooking the River Liffey. The Morrison Grill is informal, yet elegant, and the intimate Quay 14, an all-day bar-café which overlooks the River Liffey, is a great place for a cocktail. 145 rooms.

Number 31 €€€ *31 Leeson Close, Lower Leeson Street, Dublin 2, tel: 01 676 5011,* www.number31.ie. This upscale B&B, formerly home to a leading modernist architect, is a favourite with regular visitors to Dublin. It features spacious rooms, listed architecture, a sunken lounge with fireplace, and a fabulous Irish breakfast in the conservatory. 21 rooms.

The Paramount €€ *7–8 Exchange Street Upper, Temple Bar, Dublin 2; tel: 01 417 9900,* www.paramounthotel.ie. The Paramount has good rooms and a chic club feel with tobacco-tones and 1930s styling. The location, in Temple Bar is hard to beat. 64 rooms.

Premier Suites Dublin €€€ *14–17 Lower Leeson Street, Dublin 2, tel: 01 638 1111,* www.premiersuitesdublin.com. These luxurious serviced apartments are ideal for anyone planning a longer stay. Each apartment has a spacious living area with flat screen TV, music station, and broadband. 38 apartments.

Russell Court Hotel € *21–25 Harcourt Street, Dublin 2, tel: 01 478 4066,* www.russellcourthotel.ie. Two Georgian houses make up this hotel with its Victorian-style decor, plus a two-storey cottage at the rear of the hotel. Restaurant, nightclub and bars. 40 rooms.

Shelbourne Hotel €€€€ *27 St Stephen's Green, Dublin 2, tel: 01 663 4500,* www.theshelbourne.com. Dublin's most famous hotel lives up to its five-star rating. Some rooms overlook 'the Green'. A very good restaurant and two bars; try the lobby for afternoon tea. 246 rooms and 19 suites.

Staunton's on the Green €€ *83 St Stephen's Green South, Dublin 2, tel: 01 478 2300,* www.stauntonsonthegreen.ie. This exclusive Georgian guesthouse looks over St Stephen's Green in front and the Iveagh Gardens to the rear. A well-preserved historic building, with splendid high ceilings. The 40 spacious rooms are all en suite.

Temple Bar Hotel €€ *13–17 Fleet Street, Temple Bar, Dublin 2, tel: 01 677 3333,* www.templebarhotel.com. Pleasant hotel in Temple Bar, near to the bustling clubs and pubs, and a stone's throw away from shopping the havens of Grafton Street and Henry Street either side. Restaurant and bar on site. 136 rooms.

Trinity City Hotel €€ *Pearse Street, Dublin 2, tel: 01 648 1000,* www.trinitycity-hotel.com. Formerly Trinity Capital, with atmospheric Victorian decor in the lobby and bar. Bright, contemporary rooms. Mini suites have Jacuzzi baths. Restaurant. 262 rooms.

Trinity Townhouse Hotel €€ *29 South Frederick Street, Dublin 2, tel: 01 617 0900,* www.trinitytownhousehotel.com. Tucked away on a quiet side street near Trinity College, you can't get any more central than this and it's difficult to find a quieter location. Inside, the rooms have light oak furniture and big, comfy beds. 31 rooms.

The Westbury €€€€ *Balfe Street, Dublin 2, tel: 01 679 1122,* www.doylecollection.com. A favourite with visiting celebrities, the Westbury is a lush, opulent oasis just off Grafton Street. The Gallery is a favourite for afternoon tea and The Side Car is a chic spot to have a cocktail. 178 rooms and 27 suites.

The Westin €€€€ *Westmoreland Street, Dublin 2, tel: 01 645 1000,* www.thewestindublin.com. The Westin sits in a prime city centre location in one of Dublin's grandiose historic buildings. It offers everything you'd expect from an international 5-star hotel with luxurious guest rooms with all the mod cons, a fully-equipped gym and fine dining all at your fingertips. 175 rooms and 16 suites.

Wynn's Hotel €€ *35–39 Lower Abbey Street, Dublin 1, tel: 01 874 5131,* www.wynnshotel.ie. This old-fashioned city centre hotel has been a landmark since Victorian times and is just around the corner from the Abbey Theatre. This one is a favourite meeting spot for Dubliners, with a genuine local buzz, and a busy restaurant at lunch and in the early evening. There's a hotel bar, conference facilities, and rare for Dublin city centre hotels - parking. 65 rooms.

NORTH OF THE CENTRE

Bonnington Hotel €€ *Swords Road, Whitehall, Dublin 9, tel: 01 837 3544,* www.bonningtondublin.com. The Bonnington is a handy place to stay if you're coming in too late for the fun, or too early for the sun. Located between the city and the airport, the rooms are modern and the restaurant will feed you well. 200 rooms.

Egan's Guesthouse € *7–9 Iona Park, Glasnevin, Dublin 9, tel: 01 830 3611,* www.eganshouse.com. Red-brick guesthouse in a pleasant terrace of Edwardian houses, near the splendid Botanic Gardens, Croke Park and the airport. Car park. 32 rooms.

SOUTH OF THE CENTRE

Aberdeen Lodge €€€ *53–55 Park Avenue; tel: 01 283 8155; www.aberdeenlodge.com;* A large three-storey Victorian house in the elegant south Dublin area of Ballsbridge, with spacious bedrooms, beautifully furnished. Regular buses run to the centre, and it is also close to Sydney Parade DART station.

Ariel House €€ *50 Lansdowne Road; tel: 01 668 5512; www.ariel-house.net;* Elegant Victorian-style redbrick guesthouse in leafy inner suburb, with a modern wing of large comfortable bedrooms. Renowned for its breakfast.

Clayton Hotel Ballsbridge €€ *Merrion Road, Ballsbridge, Dublin 4, tel: 01 668 1111,* www.claytonhotelballsbridge.com. A spacious and modern hotel behind a restored 1793 facade, with comfortable, reasonably priced rooms, sleeping up to two adults and two children on a per room rate. The bar is a popular meeting place, and relatively quiet. Restaurant, parking. 304 rooms.

Clayton Hotel Burlington Road €€ *Upper Leeson Street, Dublin 4, tel: 01 618 5600,* www.claytonhotelburlingtonroad.com. A huge and popular hotel, this venue has Dublin's largest conference facilities. Great rates available online. Restaurants, bars, car park. 500 rooms and 6 suites.

Dylan €€€€ *Eastmoreland Place, Dublin 4, tel: 01 660 3000,* www.dylan.ie. A chic and stylish boutique hotel in a quiet location off Baggot Street, about a 15-minute walk from Grafton Street. The individually designed rooms include flat screen TVs, customised beds and underfloor-heated bathrooms. 72 rooms and suites.

Glenveagh Townhouse € *31 Northumberland Road, Ballsbridge, Dublin 4, tel: 01 668 4612*, www.glenveagh.com. A pleasant Victorian house a 15-minute walk or a short bus ride from the centre in an upmarket but fairly residential area. A quiet night's sleep is assured. Guest parking. 13 rooms.

Herbert Park Hotel and Park Residence €€ *Anglesea Road, Ballsbridge, Dublin 4, tel: 01 667 2200*, www.herbertparkhotel.ie. Stylish, comfortable, modern hotel in the Embassy district. Rooms have king-size beds. Fitness facilities. 185 rooms and 43 studio apartments.

Lansdowne Hotel €€ *27–29 Pembroke Road, Ballsbridge, Dublin 4, tel: 01 668 2522*, www.lansdownehotel.ie. This is a small, friendly family-run hotel, set back from a tree-lined road in Ballsbridge. Druid's Restaurant, traditional bar, car park. 40 rooms.

Sandymount Hotel €€ *Herbert Road, Sandymount, Dublin 4, tel: 01 614 2000*, www.sandymounthotel.ie. A family-run hotel near Lansdowne Road DART, the Aviva Stadium and Sandymount Strand (for walkers and runners). Functional but comfortable en suite rooms. Children's play area. Restaurant, bar, parking. 187 rooms.

SOUTH COAST

Fitzpatrick Castle Hotel €€–€€€ *Killiney Hill Road, Killiney, Co. Dublin, tel: 01 230 5400*, www.fitzpatrickcastle.com. This period residence sits on 3.5 hectares (9 acres) of landscaped gardens and wooded grounds, overlooking Dublin Bay. Restaurants, bar, fitness centre, swimming pool, and games room; golf, tennis and horse riding off-site. Car park. 113 rooms and suites.

Rochestown Lodge Hotel and Spa €€ *Rochestown Avenue, Dún Laoghaire, Co. Dublin, tel: 01 285 3555*, www.rochestownlodge.com. Rooms have contemporary furnishings, many with views of the Wicklow Mountains. Family rooms available. Gym and health centre. 90 rooms and suites.

INDEX

THE **MINI** ROUGH GUIDE TO
DUBLIN

First Edition 2022

Editor: Kate Drynan
Author: Philippa MacKenzie
Picture Editors: Tom Smyth & Piotr Kala
Cartography Update: Carte
Layout: Pradeep Thapliyal
Head of DTP and Pre-Press: Katie Bennett
Head of Publishing: Kate Drynan
Photography Credits: Apa Publications 32;
Kevin Cummins/Apa Publications 13; Corrie
Wingate 7T, 7B, 28, 44, 97, 105; Doug Plummer/
Apa Publications 39; Doug Plummer/Apa
Publications 58, 60, 66, 76, 79; Dublinia 46; Fáilte
Ireland 71; Glyn Genin/Apa Publications 16, 22,
26, 35, 36, 41, 42, 47, 48, 49, 51, 52, 53, 54, 57, 62,
64, 82, 84, 86, 91, 101, 103; Ireland Tourist Board
81; iStockphoto 4TC, 31; Nowitz Photography/
Apa Publications 15, 75; Public domain 6B, 18;
Shutterstock 1, 4MC, 4MC, 4TC, 4ML, 4TL, 4ML,
5T, 5M, 5M, 6T, 20, 24; 11, 69, 92, 94; Tourism
Ireland 73, 88
Cover Credits: Dublin Castle **Benoit Daoust/
Shutterstock**

Distribution

UK, Ireland and Europe: Apa Publications (UK)
Ltd; sales@roughguides.com
United States and Canada: Ingram Publisher
Services; ips@ingramcontent.com
Australia and New Zealand: Booktopia;
retailer@booktopia.com.au
Worldwide: Apa Publications (UK) Ltd;
sales@roughguides.com

Special Sales, Content Licensing and CoPublishing

Rough Guides can be purchased in bulk
quantities at discounted prices. We can create
special editions, personalised jackets and
corporate imprints tailored to your needs. sales@
roughguides.com; http://roughguides.com

Printed in Poland

This book was produced using **Typefi** automated
publishing software.

Contact us

Every effort has been made to provide accurate
information in this publication, but changes
are inevitable. The publisher cannot be held
responsible for any resulting loss, inconvenience
or injury sustained by any traveller as a result
of information or advice contained in the
guide. We would appreciate it if readers would
call our attention to any errors or outdated
information, or if you feel we've left something
out. Please send your comments with the
subject line "Rough Guide Mini Dublin Update" to
mail@k.roughguides.com.